The Psychic Workbook

The Psychic Workbook

Craig Hamilton-Parker

with Jane Hamilton-Parker

Vermilion
LONDON

Dedications

This book is dedicated to the memory of Wayne Fry and Keith Moore, two young men who fought heroic battles against cancer — and lost. Their courage in the face of adversity was like a shining light in the dark valley of death. Their victory was to prove to us all that death is not the end but a bright beginning.

First published 1995
9 10
Copyright © Craig Hamilton-Parker 1995
Craig Hamilton-Parker has asserted his moral right to
be identified as the author of this work in accordance
with the Copyright, Design and Patents Act 1988.

First published in the United Kingdom in 1995
by Vermilion an imprint of Ebury Press
Random House Group Ltd
Random House
20 Vauxhall Bridge Road
London SW1V 2SA

www.randomhouse.co.uk

Random House Australia (Pty) Ltd
20 Alfred Street, Milsons Point, Sydney,
New South Wales 2061, Australia

Random House New Zealand Limited
18 Poland Road, Glenfield,
Auckland 10, New Zealand

Random House South Africa (Pty) Limited
Endulini, 5A Jubilee Rd, Parktown 2193, South Africa

The Random House Group Limited Reg. No. 954009
A CIP catalogue record for this book is available from the British Library.
ISBN 0 09 179086 7

Designed by Jerry Goldie Graphic Design
Printed and bound in Great Britain by
Butler & Tanner Ltd, Frome and London
Papers used by Vermilion are natural, recyclable products
made from wood grown in sustainable forests.

Contents

Acknowledgements

The authors would like to thank Psychic News for their help and encouragement with the research for this book.

Introduction

This book may be one of the most important books you've ever read, particularly if you've never seriously looked at psychic subjects before.

I want it to change your life — just as psychic things changed my own life. We're going to dump the junk — dump all those negative things that have held you back — and enter a spiritual world of greater understanding and greater psychic awareness. As you progress you'll probably realize that you've intuitively known about many of the psychic gifts described all along but have never consciously expressed it. You're psychic already but just don't know it yet.

Step by step I'll explain all about how to realize your innate psychic gift. I'll be teaching you meditation and correct breathing, and instructing you about tarot, crystals, auras, psychometry, dowsing and a whole host of psychic things. But this is just the surface of what I have to say. Underlying these texts is a carefully thought-out system to attune you to your inner self — a positive, eternal self that doesn't need to worry about the petty troubles of this life. It "knows" the Truth already. Link up with your inner being and you'll not only discover your psychic abilities but you'll also become a better, more positive, more sensitive individual.

How it all began

On the eve of my sister Vivienne's wedding our grandmother had a dream. Nan dreamed that Viv was to be married in black. Everyone wore black including the bride and all the guests. To make it worse, the groom, Wayne, wasn't there. The dream was a sinister prophecy of things to come.

The wedding went off without a hitch. The young couple were very happy and were soon settled in their new home in Southampton. But a few months later dreadful news was to destroy their nuptial bliss. Wayne was diagnosed as having melanoma cancer which had spread to the liver.

You can imagine the terrible shock to us all when the doctors said there was no hope and that Wayne had only six months to live. He fought the illness with a warrior's spirit but within nine months of his diagnosis he was dead. He died in Viv's arms at home.

Viv's life was torn apart. She didn't know which way to turn and, to make it worse, Wayne's things had started to move by themselves. When Viv started smoking again, the ashtray flew across the room. Wayne had hated smoking – could he be trying to communicate?

Starting as psychics

In desperation Viv wrote a letter to the famous medium Doris Stokes. Some days later she received a phone call: "Do you understand the name Wayne, lovie?" said Doris after having introduced herself. Viv burst into tears. She had only written to ask for help and had not mentioned Wayne's name in the letter. A private sitting was arranged and a few weeks later I drove Viv to Doris's house in southwest London.

Viv and I were overwhelmed by the incredible things she said. Doris seemed to know everything about Wayne – things she could never have looked up in records. I saw the suffering drop from my sister's face. Now she could make a new start, knowing that Wayne was safe and well in the next life.

Doris Stokes then told me about my own life. "You're going through a bad patch at the moment but the future looks wonderful. You're already very psychic. I'm being told that you will be a medium like me – and there will be another that works beside you. Do you understand the name Jane Wallace? And does the 6th March mean anything to you?"

I couldn't place the name or the date but she was right about becoming a medium. It was only a few months after my sitting with Doris that I met the medium Peter Close, a retired police sergeant. He offered to train me, and within the space of two years I was to find myself able to clearly hear the spirit voices.

Jane's introduction to the psychic world was quite different. "My grandmother was very psychic," she says. "I used to stay with her as a little girl and she would encourage me to listen to the voice of my intuition. Gradually she introduced me to the crystal ball. She would plonk it in my lap and ask me what I could see. We treated it just like a game but as I grew up I began to trust my inner voice more and more."

Jane was 13 when her grandmother died. "It was one of the worst things to happen in my life. But soon after she appeared to me in a dream. She was holding a star and a glittery dress. 'You're going to be a star, and I will help you,' she said."

And she did. Now, when Jane uses her psychic gift, it is her grandmother who draws close to tell her what to say to her sitters. Just like me, and Doris Stokes before us, she too is clairaudient, or able to "hear" spirit voices.

The paths come together

Lots of couples have been brought together by match-making relatives — but few can have been introduced by a dead granny as we were.

I was giving a public demonstration of mediumship in Eastleigh, Hampshire, and the spirit of Jane's grandmother told me to speak to the 'woman in blue'.

Unbeknown to me, Jane had been receiving messages from her dead grandmother all day. She was told to go to the meeting and make sure she wore blue. Jane trusted her inner voice and went along wearing a blue dress, blue shoes, blue jewellery. When I gave the message I couldn't fail to notice her.

"I want to come to the lady in blue," I said pointing at Jane. "I hear the voice of an elderly lady and she's giving the name Barber." That was the name of Jane's grandmother, who had died 25 years earlier. "She's telling me that you too are a medium . . . and she wants you to give me a reading."

Here was a complete stranger suggesting a meeting in front of a large audience. But Jane felt that her grandmother wanted her to see me, so she agreed to a rendezvous.

"During the reading I told Craig that he would remarry and have another child," says Jane. "I had no idea that person would be me!" A whirlwind courtship followed, I proposed, Jane became pregnant with Danielle, now 5½ years old, and Jane's prediction came true.

There's a strange twist to the tale. Doris Stokes had also got it right — Jane's surname was Willis, Doris had said Wallace, and the date of our meeting . . . was the 6th of March, just as she had predicted. (We discovered much later that Jane's grandmother's maiden name was Wallace.)

"I often wonder if Doris watched the wedding from the hereafter," says Jane. "I'd become good friends with her husband, John Stokes, after Doris died in 1987. And it was John who gave me away in church!"

Fame strikes

Jane and I decided to combine our psychic skills. We gave public demonstrations, hosted a regular radio show and began writing for magazines. But our big break came when Bob Geldof's new TV company heard of us and invited us to appear on The Big Breakfast as the resident psychics.

It was the weirdest job interview we'd ever had. Jane and I gave psychic consultations to the producers. One of them was so shocked by our accuracy that he had to take some time off to think over what we had said.

"The first show was the hardest," says Jane. "Nobody knew if The Big Breakfast was going to work. It was a hectic schedule. And our job was the worst of all: we had to predict next week's news."

By the time we finished our six months of weekly slots, everybody was asking us for advice. Even The Big Breakfast presenter Paula Yates softened her attitude when we did our stuff on a Friday morning.

We predicted the death of the Queen's favourite corgi, the El Al air tragedy, and the birth of "miracle" Siamese twins. Each week we would hold up the newspaper headlines. Jane predicted that Princess Anne would get married — and she even named the venue and best man!

Chris Evans was the first to interview us. I think that he thought that we were a couple of lunatics. But soon his attitude changed and he was singing our praises. He even admitted that his mother was a bit psychic.

On Fridays Paula Yates would interview celebrities in her "boudoir" and Jane and I would share a dressing room with the stars. It was amazing to casually meet so many famous people. We were walking in another world.

I was surprised how many celebrities were interested in psychic things. It's well known that actors are superstitious but many of them have a real insight into the world of the paranormal. Some of the stars we met on set included: Patrick Swayzee, Frank Bruno, Chris Eubank, Naomi Campbell, Oliver Reed, Tom Jones, Kylie Minogue, Jason Donovan, Glenda Jackson, Billy Joe Spears, Rupert Everett, Brother Beyond and Take That. Now we could name-drop at parties. You'll read about some of the stars' intriguing psychic stories later.

The Future

The Big Breakfast appreciated our input into the show. Nobody had ever expected that the show would be such a mega-success. Our association with them meant that the press and other TV shows were eager to hear what we had to say.

Soon we were appearing on all sorts of TV programmes and were flown all over the country to talk about and demonstrate our psychic gifts. Our hopes for the future are that we can expand our work to an international stage. Perhaps the predictions made about us by others, which seemed so unrealistic at the time, are coming to pass.

But Jane and I like to keep our feet firmly on the ground. Even though we have a special gift, we believe that this is not something unique to us. *Everybody is psychic to a greater or lesser degree.* In this book I'll show you how to unlock your own psychic powers and how the stars have sometimes unlocked theirs.

Chapter 1

Psychic Powers

Psychic abilities can broadly be broken down into four categories. We'll go into these in more detail later but here they are, as a taster for what's to come:

❖ **Telepathy**   The ability to "tune in" to the thoughts of others or to inject your own thoughts into another's mind.

❖ **Clairvoyance**   The acquisition of information which is not available to you by the known senses and which is not known by anyone else.

❖ **Precognition**   Knowledge about events before they take place, enabling you to make predictions about the future.

❖ **Psychokinesis**   The power of the mind to influence matter, for example moving objects by thought.

Perhaps you've already experienced some psychic abilities in your ordinary life. How many of the following questions can you answer with a "yes"?

The psychic 'IQ' test

1 Do you win at board games that involve chance and even occasionally will a double-six to fall? Do electrical gadgets like photocopiers go wrong when you are angry or upset?

2 Do you finish people's sentences for them or know what they are going to say next?

3 Do you sometimes take an instant dislike to someone you've only just been introduced to, without really knowing why? And do animals, which are very sensitive to psychic powers, either love you or hate you for no reason?

4 Have you ever tried to ring a friend only to find that their line is engaged because they were trying to phone you at the same time? Or do you sometimes know who's at the other end of the phone before you answer your calls?

5 Have you ever smelled tobacco, flowers or perfume when there's no apparent cause? Or perhaps heard a loud knock and later discovered that an acquaintance had died at that moment?

6 Have you ever dreamed of dead relatives and been told by them things that you later found out were true?

7 Have you ever dreamed of flying, or travelled outside of your body in a dream, or "seen" an event taking place miles away?

8 Do you sometimes see coloured lights around people's heads?

9 Have you ever seen spirit people or had an imaginary friend as a child? Do you still hold conversations with a departed loved one?

10 Have you ever been so influenced by a dream that it has made you alter your plans? Do you sense danger moments before it happens or have disaster dreams that come true?

There will be a large number of people reading this that can answer in the affirmative to most or all of the above questions. Even if you find that only some of the questions strike a chord, there is raw material that we can work with.

The qualities that make a good psychic

What makes some people more psychic than others? These are not hard and-fast rules but some may apply to you.

❖ **Personality**   Are you bright and bubbly? ESP experiments have concluded that outgoing, extrovert personalities score better results in tests than sombre, reflective types.

❖ **Sensitivity**   Are you easily hurt? Psychics are extremely sensitive individuals and will often be influenced by other people's moods. You may even be able to tell if someone's in a bad mood before you see their face.

❖ **Creativity**   Are you artistic? A large proportion of psychics come from an artistic background. Some researchers believe that this is because psychics, like artists, predominantly use the righthand side of the brain — the side that's responsible for intuition.

❖ **Dreams**   Do you have vivid dreams? Dreams are a direct route to the subconscious mind. If you're in tune with your inner self then you become in tune with your psychic self. Psychic experiences are most likely to happen when your mind and body are relaxed and receptive.

❖ **Perceptions**   Do you see bright lights around living things? If so, then you can see the aura which is a magnetic field that changes with our moods. You are very psychic. Also you may have a greater awareness of colour than most people.

❖ **Intuition** Do you trust your intuition? Much of the information we get through intuition is gained clairvoyantly. If you finish people's sentences for them, you may be picking up their thoughts by telepathy. Women trust their intuition more than men: 85 per cent of people who report paranormal events are women.

Strange psychic stories of the stars

It's important to remind ourselves that the psychic gift is not necessarily the gift of only the few. You'd be surprised how many well-known people believe in psychic skills. Throughout these chapters I'll give you a few examples of famous people who have had a psychic experience. You may not know these people personally but you know enough about them to realize that psychic experiences can happen to all sorts of very different personality types.

Are you psychic?

The great modern-day medium Gordon Higginson used to say, "Mediums are born, they're not made." He was right, but the best mediums and psychics have also trained their natural gift and thereby transformed it into something extraordinary. Many of the psychic skills outlined here can be mastered by most open-minded novices.

Are you psychic? No? Well, you may be more psychic than you think. Let's consider some

---

STRANGE PSYCHIC STORIES OF THE STARS

Spike Milligan

Comedian and author Spike Milligan was brought up in India but never took an interest in the psychic practitioners all around him – until a strange event changed his mind. One day, while listening to a football match on the radio, he was annoyed when his watch stopped at 4.20pm. He went into his kitchen to adjust his watch and found that the kitchen clock had also stopped at 4.20pm. Then the phone rang. He answered it and heard the speaking clock saying it was 4.20 and 18 seconds. This shocked Spike, so he dialled the telephone engineers, who explained that it was impossible and such a thing had never happened before. The next morning, Spike received a sad letter. His beloved grandmother had died the previous day at 4.20pm.

psychic experiences that you may have already had. When you first bought a house or rented a room did you ever say, "This place *feels* right"? It may have been similar to other properties, you may not have liked the decoration or the colours, but something about the place told you that it was just right. Why did you feel this way? Was it intuition or was it something much deeper? You may have been using a latent psychic skill to sense the building's atmosphere.

The cerebral cortex of the brain is divided into two hemispheres and joined by a large bundle of interconnected nerve fibres called the corpus callosum. In effect, we have two different brains that work in harmony with one another to produce the sum total of what we are. The lefthand brain controls the righthand side of the body and is responsible for our reason. It also is predominantly involved with logical thinking, especially in verbal and mathematical functions. It thinks in sequences and forms categories.

It is from the brain's righthand side that we gain our intuitive skills. The righthand side of the brain controls the lefthand side of the body. Instead of thinking in categories, it sees things as a whole. This hemisphere is responsible for our artistic abilities, our body image and our ability to recognize faces. When we get a gut feeling of the answer to a problem, it is our righthand brain that is giving us the solution. This intuitive side of ourselves is often grossly neglected. Society wants logical, rational thinkers and ignores this other half of ourselves. Intuition is not a whimsical female preoccupation but an essential mental function and, if fully developed, can lead to remarkable psychic abilities.

Most people are psychic to some degree but they either pay little attention to it or don't even realize they are using a sixth sense in the first place. Psychics believe that thoughts are not limited to chemical processes in the brain but can travel outside of ourselves. And just like a radio receiver, a sensitive person can "tune in" to these vibrations.

Telepathy, which is the communication of

Michael Bentine

Michael Bentine, the 70-year-old star of theatre, television and radio, has been a believer in the paranormal all his life. He spoke of his father's work as a psychic researcher. "My father was deeply involved with the paranormal. He used children in experiments" – including the young Michael Bentine.

Bentine claims to have had many psychic experiences himself including a premonition that his 21-year-old son would die in a plane crash. "I knew my son would die, and Andy, the boy with him, if they flew together." Michael tried to warn them but his precognition proved "horribly true".

(P N 1 7 J u l y 9 3)

thoughts between two people, works best when you fall in love. The barriers come down and thoughts flow freely between you. You probably have already experienced this but didn't recognize it as a psychic experience. The telepathic empathy between lovers expresses itself when both say the same thing at the same time or finish each other's sentences. Love – and telepathy – know no barriers, and the one you love may sense your thoughts even when there are many miles between you.

The same thing is true between mothers and their newborn babies. Psychologists have found that if a sleeping baby is put into a soundproof room, in many cases the mother will know when the child has woken up and starts crying even though there is no way she could have heard the baby's cries. Again, it's the loving thoughts between mother and child that make this form of telepathy possible.

The psychic gifts nature has given us have a protective role also: the sixth sense will warn us if somebody we meet may mean us harm. That's why sometimes we take an instant dislike to some people. We feel their vibrations and our intuition tells us to watch them.

Tribal people are still aware of these now forgotten skills. Telepathic communication over long distances is commonplace. They also believe that some places are sacred or dangerous depending on the vibrations of that area. The land itself warns or encourages us. Perhaps warning signals are telepathically left on the ether, imprinted for future generations. The aborigines of Australia believe in a network of invisible pathways, and it has been their religious duty for 20,000 years to walk these tracks singing their ancient songs and paying homage to their ancestors. They enter a state of consciousness called "Dream Time" where they merge with the ancient knowledge of their ancestors and the forces of animals, creeks, rocks, birds, insects and waterholes. There is so much that we too can learn from our long forgotten past. Ancient skills are waiting to be reanimated.

The unseen man

When a human egg develops it goes through a metamorphosis from a few simple cells to a complete baby. In the many stages inbetween, we witness within the developing embryo the whole genetic evolution of man compressed into a time span of about nine months. It's like 3000 million years of history on fast forward. The foetus at about three weeks old even has gills like a fish! His cells divide, specializing to become tissue, nerves, liver, heart, brain, and other organs. The DNA even has encoded within it patterns of behaviour to help us survive the harsh and hazardous environment that lies ahead, outside of the comforting embryonic waters. Most of our inherited behaviour patterns are obsolete and are no longer necessary for survival in the modern world. Yet they still lie dormant in the unconscious, ready to reanimate should they be needed again (if they were, for example, another Ice Age or if dinosaurs began roaming the earth once more). Mankind is an ancient being and evolution's long memory is locked away within each of us.

Below the thin layer of brain called the cerebral cortex, where the rational mind functions, lies the 90 per cent of our being that we are unaware of: the primitive, reptilian brain of centuries long gone. It's my belief that archaic man thought and used his perceptions in a completely different way to us and that the psychic functions are nothing new but were once part of our day-to-day consciousness. They will, one day, rise to reclaim the throne within the human psyche. It is possible, with effort, to fathom those deep wells and draw from the ancient knowledge of prehistory. One of those lost treasures is extra-sensory perception.

Nature experiments with evolution. Some strains of evolving man have died out. Similarly, some of man's mental functions stayed for a time and then went backstage to wait for the next call to perform. The time has come to reawaken our latent perceptions.

Trust your intuition, as your psychic awareness may well be guiding you or telling you of future problems and opportunities. Archaic man is alive and well and living within each of us.

Not only are thoughts able to travel outside of ourselves but they can travel through time as well. When you felt that atmosphere of place when buying a house, your psychic senses were giving you, just like the aborigines, a glimpse of the past. In the same way you can use your sixth sense to get a glimpse of your potential future; dreams can be the tool to do this. In sleep the psychic senses work through the subconscious, whose language is symbols, metaphors and images. In the pages that follow you will be taught a diverse range of techniques to enable you to unlock all of these latent talents.

The case for ESP

Nothing infuriates traditional scientists more than claims of the paranormal. Levitation, spoon bending, life after death and telepathy threaten the whole fabric of science. Sceptical committees, set up to investigate claims, invariably conclude that the phenomena are fake. They resent serious paranormal experimentation for, if confirmed, the established basis of science would be threatened. Many prominent scientists refuse even to investigate the evidence.

Despite this antagonistic environment there remain a few scientists with the courage to investigate ESP and also face the scorn and derision of their colleagues. One notable example was the early pioneer of parapsychology, Joseph Rhine, from Harvard University.

Rhine was the person who coined the term ESP or extra sensory perception. Despite popular misuse, ESP has a specific meaning: it refers to any mental faculty that allows a person to acquire information about the world without the use of the known senses. This includes telepathy, clairvoyance, precognition and psychokinesis.

Psychic experiment

Telepathy using Zener cards

In 1930 Rhine and his colleague Karl Zener hit upon a simple but brilliant idea to measure ESP, and telepathy in particular. They designed a set of cards now known as Zener cards. Each pack consists of 25 cards of five different symbols: a black square, green star, red cross, orange circle and blue wavy lines. The cards are shuffled by the "sender" and then turned over one by one. Then the "receiver", or "percipient", situated in another room or building, has to identify each card and make a note of the images seen. Rhine would repeat the experiments again and again, to reduce the possibility of chance affecting the outcome. He achieved some startling results. You can conduct a similar experiment.

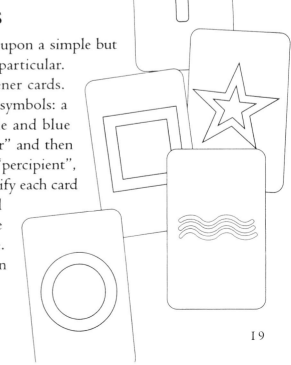

1 First cut out the cards printed at the back of this book. Select someone to be the "sender" and another to be the "receiver". Sit in different rooms and both quieten your minds and imagine an indigo blue light shining in your forehead. This is the psychic centre, nicknamed the "third eye".

2 The sender then shuffles the cards and concentrates on its image for about three minutes. The receiver should try to visualize the image and write it down. It's best to trust the first image you see. Don't keep changing your mind – go with your gut feeling, as the first thought that comes to you is probably right. If your psychic centre is open, you will see a picture in your forehead – in your "mind's eye". The poet W B Yeats, who was a member of the magical group The Golden Dawn, practised a similar technique with symbolic cards.

3 The sender mustn't talk about the cards, even if the rooms are far apart, or the receiver may unconsciously hear the words. When the sender has finished, they should ring a bell or clap their hands so that the receiver knows that another image is about to be transmitted.

4 After a run of 25 cards, compare notes. You may be surprised at the results.

An above-average score may indicate that telepathy has taken place between two people. However, Rhine, and other researchers after him, noticed something very strange. Results sometimes showed that the receivers were getting it right except that they were out of sequence by one card. They were *anticipating* the next card before the sender had looked at it. The borderline between clairvoyance and telepathy is very thin indeed. Because of this, let's try another simple experiment before we consider Rhine and Zener's results.

Psychic experiment

Clairvoyance using Zener cards

1 For this experiment lay all 25 cards face down in front of you and touch each one in turn. Try to visualize which card it is.

2 When you feel right, turn it over. Make a note of how many you get right. Don't be disheartened if you get some wrong — it's been proved that the more confident you remain, the greater are the chances of getting it right. Keep your notes because in Chapter 5 we'll try a similar experiment using a pendulum. It will be interesting to see just how much your psychic abilities improve as you read this book.

3 Now check your result.

Pure chance would give you a result of a maximum of five right. More than this and you may be showing signs of ESP. Shuffle the cards and try again; if you consistently score above average, then you are remarkably psychic.

Putting psychics to the test

Rhine established some astonishing results when he put psychics to the test. Psychic Hubert E Pearce was asked to guess the sequence of Zener cards being transmitted by Rhine's assistant, Joseph Pratt. He would pick the cards up, at intervals of one minute, without looking at them. Pearce would then write down his guesses. The experiments were carefully monitored and the subjects were situated in different buildings to eliminate potential fraud.

Even Rhine was amazed at the results: Pearce scored ten hits out of every 25 cards dealt — over double the odds that chance would have yielded. How do your results compare with this?

The science of parapsychology

These early psychic experiments laid the foundation stone that established parapsychology as a valid science. Recent experiments have become more imaginative, with forced-choice targets like Zener cards replaced by free-response targets. The sender is put in a setting and the psychic describes where they are. Here are a few notable examples.

In 1978 Hella Hammid described an airport control tower as "a square tower with leaf-like protrusions around it . . . Something mechanical, something that needs to be visible from the sky . . . like . . . an airport tower."

Another subject described the Louisiana Superdome as "a large circular building with a white dome . . . resembling a flying saucer in the middle of the city". These were exactly the same words that the sender had dictated into his tape recorder.

One of the largest ESP experiments was conducted by the rock group The Grateful Dead at one of their New York concerts in 1971. The audience was shown an image for 15 minutes and asked to mentally transmit the picture to English psychic Malcolm Bessent, who was asleep 50 miles away. Bessent's dreams contained four out of the six weird images sent to him.

Serious scientific studies still continue. Edinburgh University now has a chair of parapsychology set up from a bequest made by the author Arthur Koestler. Charles Honerton, who worked there, set up a series of studies recently with Daryl Bem, a professor of psychology from Cornell University in New York. Professor Bem said that he had been a magician since he was 17 but had moved on to a study of true phenomena, which he refers to as "mentalism".

In the experiments, the sender concentrated on an art print or film clip and the receiver recorded the feelings, thoughts and images that emerged. There was a 25 per cent probability of a hit occurring by pure chance.

When the results were brought together the hit rate proved to be about 33 per cent, which was statistically significant. Film clips revealed an even higher rate – 40 per cent – and if the subjects were friends they achieved hit rates that were better still. Professor Bem believes that his technique of "meta-analysis" is the most persuasive evidence yet for extra-sensory perception, claiming that "the probability of the results occurring by chance was less than one in a billion".

STRANGE PSYCHIC STORIES OF THE STARS

Joan Rivers

Seeing an event at a distance is known as remote viewing. In some cases the experience is so powerful that the subject leaves their physical body and travels in their "etheric double" (an astral duplicate of the physical body, which survives death). The American chat show hostess Joan Rivers has claimed to have travelled out of her body. She says that she "flew" to California, where her daughter lived. "I saw my daughter in the shower – I rang her immediately to confirm what happened – and that's exactly what she had just been doing."

Let's get started

If you're anything like me, you've been straining at the leash to start your psychic work from the moment that you bought this book. So before we start going into detail, why not give these simple psychic experiments a try to get you started?

Psychometry

The thoughts that we project are absorbed by objects we have owned for a long period of time. Using your psychic intuition, it is possible to "replay" these recordings. The psychic ability to tell the history of an object and its owner is called psychometry.

1 Ask a friend to lend you a small object such as a watch or ring, belonging to someone they know. The history of the object should be known by your friend but unknown to you. We're going to try to describe the life and character of the object's owner.

2 Relax and allow your intuitive thinking to flow. It is important not to worry about making mistakes at this stage. Say exactly what comes into your head without trying to censor or interpret the images that you see. Hold the object and just let the words flow. What is the first thing you feel? Is this a warm person or a cold, insensitive person? Is this person a worrier? Are they happy or sad? Shy or extrovert? What do they like: sport, art, discos, walking, food? Silently ask yourself questions and answer them as you speak.

3 Dig below the surface. It's important not to be too influenced by what you see in front of you. A Scorpio pendant may have been owned by an Aquarian; a Sonic the Hedgehog keyring may have been bought for granny by her grandchildren; the owner of a flash watch may be broke. Talk about what you feel, not what you see with your eyes.

4 Start with simple things and then try to build up a picture of the owner.

Your friend listening should remain quiet until you have finished. Ask yourself about the person's past. Were they happy as a child? Have they travelled a great deal? Perhaps they are a loner? The important thing is to keep talking and let your intuitive self take control. But don't make predictions – it's the provable facts that we're interested in.

5 When you feel you have finished, ask your friend to tell you what percentage you got right. Ask them also about specific things you may have said. Psychometry is a psychic ability that most people can develop with practice. You may really surprise yourself with your accuracy!

P s y c h i c   e x p e r i m e n t

Prediction

Why not put the adverts on TV to good use to develop your powers of prediction? Try guessing, when viewing with your family, what advert is going to appear next. Start simply – for example, "I think the next advert will be for cat or dog food" – then try to get more specific by naming the product.

P s y c h i c   e x p e r i m e n t

Telepathy

1 Decide who is going to be the sender and who the receiver. Sit quietly in different rooms and imagine a bright light opening in your "third eye" in the middle of the forehead.

2 The sender now draws a simple picture. If you are the receiver you must watch the images appearing in your mind's eye. Draw the first thing you see. As with psychometry you mustn't censor your thoughts – go with the flow.

3 When finished, compare drawings and see how close you got.

The best images to communicate telepathically involve all the senses and emotions, so when its your turn to send the image, remember to transmit as emotional a picture as you can, bringing in all the senses. For example, a painful image of a hand being hit by a hammer involves sight, touch and sound.

Psychic experiment

Remote viewing

1 This experiment involves a "sleeping partner". Ask a friend, who that evening will be sleeping in a different room or house, to put an unusual object, such as a cornflake packet or a child's toy, on their dressing table before they go to bed.

2 When you awake in the morning, write down your dream or the first thing that comes into your head.

3 Check later if your dream includes the object they chose. Your subconscious may distort the image: if, for example, they chose a child's toy you may that night have dreamed of children, or if it was a cereal packet you may have dreamed of eating. Keep trying the experiments, and the pictures that come to you will become more specific.

How did you fare? Whatever the results, remember that you've only taken your first step. In the next chapter, we'll start looking at psychic development in a bit more detail.

STRANGE PSYCHIC STORIES OF THE STARS

Barbara Woodhouse

Barbara Woodhouse, the famous TV animal-trainer, was convinced that a telepathic bond existed between humans and pets. "I have always been able to understand and read their thoughts. They come on my brain just as if they were speaking my language. It is what we send out to them that matters. It goes out in waves. I feel the waves of love coming back."

She didn't realize that her telepathic gifts were unusual. "I thought everyone could do it," she said. "I was quite surprised when I found people did not hear what their dogs were thinking."

She also believed that animals survived death. "If people say dogs have no souls," she said at a literary luncheon, 'I reply, `Then you have no soul yourself.'

(P N 2 3 / 7 / 8 8)

Chapter 2

Meditation

The key to psychic development is meditation.

I t may sound like a tedious pastime but once you've begun to master some of these very simple techniques it'll become one of your favourite activities. Psychic powers are not the only fruits of meditation; peace of mind, increased IQ and memory, relaxation, good health, creativity and self-confidence are just a few of the others. Meditation attunes you to your higher self and imbues your life with spirituality. The rewards are great, yet it's dead simple to do.

The millennium gurus

Indian gurus and teachers have, over the last 50 years, brought to the West's attention the 5000-year-old Eastern traditions of meditation. Introduced by remarkable teachers like Gurdgieff, Yogananda and Krishnamurti, meditation and yoga have become accessible to everyone. When in the 1960s the Beatles visited Maharishi Yogi's ashram in India, meditation, and in particular transcendental meditation, became front page news. George Harrison also popularized the Hari Krishna movement, founded by Bhaktivedanta Swami Prabhupada, and donated a substantial sum of money to build their headquarters.

Today the most prominent Indian teacher is Sathya Sai Baba. He is considered an Avatar, which is the Eastern equivalent of the second coming.

Sai Baba has millions of followers worldwide yet has never travelled outside of India.

His attraction is that he is a miracle worker. Jane and I have spoken to reliable people who have witnessed incredible things. One of our good friends was cured of total paralysis and others have seen him materialize objects out of thin air. One friend told of a medallion that materialized around his own neck. It contained a profile picture of Sai Baba that, over the years, has turned to become a frontal view.

A friend gave us some of Sai Baba's materialized healing ash, called vibuti, which we gave to a friend of ours who was dying. He didn't recover but the room filled with a beautiful smell of jasmine and our friend died peacefully soon after seeing the orange-clad, fuzzy-haired form of Sai Baba materialize in his room.

Like all of the great teachers before him, Sai Baba teaches the importance of meditation in spiritual development.

The simple way to spiritual truth

Despite its high profile, meditation is still a mystery to many. The problem is that there are so many different techniques. Some use a mantra, which is an Indian holy phrase that the yogi inwardly repeats over and over again.

Other methods involve watching the breath or contemplating an object. Mandalas and yantras, circular designs that symbolize the unity of existence, are also used as a meditation focus. Japanese Zen meditation requires the monks to contemplate a Koan — an impossible statement that bypasses the reason to trigger self-realization. A typical set problem to solve is, "What is the sound of one hand clapping?" Understand it and enlightenment could be yours.

Clearly there are many paths to the mountaintop, and different systems will appeal to different temperaments. In the exercises that follow I've tried to make meditation as accessible as possible by looking at only the simplest, but arguably the most effective, techniques. In this chapter we'll focus on methods to still the mind, relieve stress and increase pranic energy — the body's life force. If you want to develop your psychic skills, meditation is the most powerful tool you can use. Later in the chapter meditation methods targeted at clairvoyant development are explained.

The instant stress buster

Stress is the biggest killer today. In the East they believe that our bodies are revitalized by a life energy called prana. Breathing techniques can stimulate this healing energy and promote better health and peace of mind.

Try this simple exercise. Loosen tight clothing and sit somewhere quiet and comfortable. Let your breathing gradually become slow and deep. Next, when you inhale tell yourself, "I am" and when you exhale "relaxed". Repeat this a few times. When you say the word "relaxed" to yourself, let your body slowly sink deeper into the chair. This exercise, which takes only a few minutes, will slow the heart rate and raise body temperature — physiological changes that signify a relaxed state.

Breath control

Pranic energy, unlike oxygen, can be accumulated in the etheric body. The breath is the key to increasing this life energy, which will improve your vitality and supply the fuel that drives your psychic and healing powers. Prana is the vital link between the physical and astral bodies. Here are two simple techniques:

Pranic breathing

With all breathing techniques and yoga, it is important never to force results. If at any stage you begin to feel discomfort or start to sweat, you've missed the point. We're looking to achieve a restful state and to gently fill yourself with pranic energy. If in doubt, stop.

I   Sit in a comfortable posture. Yogis sit cross-legged on the floor but, so long as the spine is straight, a chair will do. Take a deep breath and exhale through the mouth with a sigh. Relax as you exhale. Do it two more times. Now breathe normally for a while.

2   Close your eyes. Focus your attention on your breathe but at this stage just breath normally. Now visualize the air entering your nose as being made of white light. See it stream into your lungs and fill them with radiant light. You feel revitalized and full of energy.

3   As you breathe out, see the air coming out of your nostrils as black arid smoke. You are inhaling pranic light and exhaling all the impurities of the body and mind.

4   If you slow the breath down, the pranic energy is increased. Now inhale slowly, taking a deep unhurried breath, but don't cram the lungs with air to the point of discomfort. Concentrate your full attention onto what you are doing. Think of the lungs as being composed of lower, middle and upper spaces. Fill the bottom part first, then the middle and finally the top.

5   Hold the breath for two or three seconds and release the air slowly through the nostrils. Make a thorough slow exhalation, pause for two or three seconds then start another inhalation. The whole process should be gentle and relaxed. If you feel you want to gulp for air, you're trying to progress too quickly.

6   In the early stages, between five and ten breaths are quite sufficient to revitalize your pranic energy. Gradually you can increase the length and number of breaths as you become more accustomed to the technique.

7   Once you've mastered the basic technique and can hold your concentration on the breath, try it again and visualize the air inhaled as light and exhaled as smoke. Fill your whole body with light energy.

Storing psychic energy

Just below the rib cage is located a complex of nerves, called the solar plexus. It is an important chakra – a psychic centre. When you do your breathing exercise, imagine this centre filling with the light of the breath and retaining the energy. The solar plexus is your psychic battery; it stores the pranic energy. I'll explain how to use this energy later in the book.

As you hold your breath, stockpile the prana. The solar plexus will become warm as you do this. It is also a useful exercise in mind control. If you direct the attention and focus the prana to damaged or diseased parts of your own or another's body (by the laying on of hands), the prana acts as a healing agent.

Practise this exercise daily.

Inner peace

To be in tune with your psychic abilities, you must first get in tune with yourself. You may think that meditation has very little to do with psychic skills but in fact it is the single most important aid to your development. Also, it's a real treat. Inner peace is the greatest reward we could ever expect to gain from life.

The brain never stops talking: yap, yap, yap. The internal dialogue never stops: yap, yap, yap. And there's nothing much you can do about it. You can't force yourself to stop thinking but you can step aside and just watch the thoughts. This, in essence, is what meditation is all about.

In daily life our thoughts rush hither and thither. In meditation we focus them and reduce them so that the light of the inner self can shine. And it's at times when our mind is still that we can recognize the impressions we receive from our sixth sense.

The mind is like a glass of muddy water. The more you shake it, the worse it gets. But if you leave it alone the mud settles to the bottom and the water becomes crystal-clear. It's the same with meditation. We stand back and the mud, our thoughts, settles leaving our consciousness crystal-clear.

There are three simple steps to meditation: relaxation, interiorization and meditation.

Relaxation exercises

Stand up. Take a deep breath. Put both hands above your head and stretch your whole body as if you've just woken from a deep sleep. Then let your whole body relax totally.

Sit in a comfortable chair, making sure that your spine is erect, the chest up and the shoulders slightly back. Breathe gently from the diaphragm.

Now consciously relax the whole body. Start with the feet and work your way up, part by part, to the head and brain.

Interiorization exercises

The breathing techniques you've tried have helped fix your attention. Simply watching the slow rising and falling of the breath fixes the attention inwards. It stills the thoughts and focuses the mind. Breathe gently. Feel the breath as it passes in and out of the nostrils. If you find this difficult, focus on the movement of the chest and lungs then transfer your awareness back to the nostrils. Watching the breath is one of the central and most important techniques of yoga: as the breath quietens so does the mind.

Once the breath is calm, you can transfer your attention from the breath to the point between the eyebrows. This chakra, nicknamed the third eye, is the centre of your will. It directs the flow of prana, and by concentrating on this you interiorize your prana, energy. The deeper your concentration, the calmer your breath becomes. Your life force has become focused on the spiritual self.

You can continue in this state for as long as you like. It wipes away your worries and induces a deep inner calm. (Try it before you visit the dentist.)

Some people complain that their thoughts don't quieten at all when they sit to meditate — they speed up. But what is really happening is that these people are becoming more aware of just how hectic their normal thinking is. In time the thoughts will quieten down as they master this simple method.

Sarah Miles

Actress Sarah Miles is a regular meditator. She says that it distracts her from the greed, lust and ambition of this world. "First you have to concentrate on your breathing. Then you get to the 'no' thoughts position: it can take a year to eliminate mundane thoughts like "Have I washed out my knickers?" Joking aside, Sarah Miles is making a spiritual effort to build a bridge between the "lower" and "higher" selves.

Meditation techniques

Once your breath has quietened and you have focused on the third-eye centre, you are ready to step into the next stages of meditation. You are at the control board of your own biological computer — the mind. You can now practise a variety of meditative techniques. Try one per session and find out which suits you best.

Light visualization

Visualization bypasses the internal verbal dialogue. Sometimes visions will occur spontaneously, but by consciously visualizing we build a bridge to the super-conscious.

You may want to imagine a picture of a beautiful scene, such as walking through a pastoral valley with lush trees, crystal waterfalls and singing birds. Some imagine the face of their guru or Christ shedding love on them.

See a white light in your third-eye centre growing brighter and brighter. Imagine it filling your whole body like liquid light, filling first the toes and feet then the legs and trunk. Fill the hands and arms, the chest and right up to the very top of the head. Your body is like a chalice filled with light.

Now imagine the whole world filling with light. The room you're sitting in, your town or city, the country, the world becomes light. Then expand this to include the solar system, galaxy and universe. See infinite light above you, below you, to the left and right, in front and behind. You are a being of light floating in an infinite sea of light. Now merge your light with the infinite light, just like the line in Sir Edwin Arnold's poem, "The Dewdrop slips into the shining Sea".

This is a tremendously powerful technique, which is also very effective when practised as a group, with one person talking the others through the visualization. It brings you close to the ultimate goal of meditation: realization of the infinite light of God, which has been described by Indian holy texts as "the light of ten thousand Suns with the stillness of ten thousand Moons".

Sound visualization

Many meditation techniques use sound as a focus to still the mind. The simplest method is to listen with all your attention to some gentle music.

Psychologists have found that the brain patterns of subjects listening to structured music such as Mozart's are similar to the patterns displayed by people playing chess. They argue that listening to music can increase intelligence.

Similarly, electroencephalograms (EEGs) taken of meditators who use a mantra (the inward repetition of a holy phrase) show an increased level of alpha, theta and delta brain waves — signs that the meditators are in a deep state of peace.

Maharishi Yogi's Transcendental Meditation (TM) instructs students to repeat inwardly a mantra, the words of which are different for each student. The Hari Krishna movement does the same and you will hear their saffron-robed devotees chanting their mantra in London's Oxford Street. But you don't have to shave your head or become part of a sect to practise a mantra.

One of the most ancient mantras is the Sanskrit word "om" (pronounced "aum"). This can be chanted aloud or, better still (and the neighbours will appreciate this), verbalized inwardly. Like the Christian word "amen", it is representative of the divinity of God. In this, instead of filling the world with light, you harmonize with the universal sound of creation. The word must be sounded as one syllable only. It can be as long or as short as you like. The "m" sound will be at least twice as long as the "o" ("au") sound, which should be full and round, as in the word "home". The "m" tapers off like the sound of a bell, gradually fading away. For example, the "o" may last for about two seconds and the "m" for about four. First try chanting the word out loud, then say it inwardly. Try to unite with the sound and feel it echo throughout the vastness of the universe. This technique will expand your consciousness and bring you closer to the psychic part of yourself.

Another technique, recommended by the yogis, which considerably increases clairvoyant skills, is to listen to the sounds of the inner ear. This technique has to be practised either late at night or in a completely

STRANGE PSYCHIC STORIES OF THE STARS

Omar Sharif

While filming in Bulgaria, film star Omar Sharif was doubled over with pain because of a stomach ulcer. Then the producer's wife, actress Betty Bolvary, told him that she was a spiritual healer.

"At first I scoffed at her," admitted Omar, "but she insisted, asking me to give her just one minute. Gripped by pain, I thought, 'What will one minute cost me?' So I agreed."

After Betty had finished, Omar Sharif had changed his tone: "I realized in that moment that the pain had gone. There was not even the slightest twinge. In 60 seconds I had been cured."

(PN 26/12/87)

soundless environment. You will have noticed that if you've been listening to very loud music, you are left with an unpleasant ringing in your ears. However, under less severe conditions it is possible to perceive this ringing as soothing. When you sit for meditation, listen to this inner sound. You will notice that each ear's sound is slightly different and a resonance is created. Switch the attention from one ear to the other and let your thoughts dissolve into the resulting resonance. You may also hear your own heartbeat, and with prolonged practice, the yogis say, you will hear sounds like reed pipes, bells and gongs. This attentive technique is claimed to greatly increase clairvoyant powers.

Mantras and listening to the inner ear fix the thoughts. A simple "New Age" technique is to substitute a mantra by slowly counting backwards from 100 to 0, intoned inwardly. Scientific tests have shown that by doing this, particularly if the closed eyes are raised upwards at an angle of 20 degrees, the brain emits more alpha waves, a sign of deep relaxation.

STRANGE PSYCHIC STORIES OF THE STARS

Richard Harris

Film star Richard Harris has been haunted twice. In November 1969 he said that he had filled a room of his house with toys. He had been hearing weird noises in that room and believed they "were from the ghost of a child. I thought the toys would help the ghost to be happy and it seemed to do the trick." Researching the history of the house, he discovered that a child had died in the room with the noises. Three years later he bought a 100-year-old house in Kensington, London. He heard a child crying in the loft, the piano playing by itself in the lounge and footsteps in the minstrels' gallery. Once a woman walked past and vanished into thin air. But Richard got used to the phantoms: "Now I would not be without my ghosts. I have grown accustomed to them."

(PN 26/12/87)

Watching the thoughts

"Sitting quietly doing nothing, Spring comes, and the grass grows by itself," says the famous Japanese poem. Zen meditation believes in a spontaneous realization of the absolute. The ultimate answer to life and the universe is so simple that the mind cannot grasp it. It's beyond the mind.

Simply observing the thoughts frees us from the endless thinking process. Just as you watched the breath you can do the same with your own mind. In your meditation, watch the thoughts that come to you. Observe them but do not follow them. If you find that you have slipped and fallen into a stream of thinking, bring yourself back to the third-eye centre and start again. You mustn't try to suppress thoughts. Simply observe them and then let them go. You are watching yourself.

Sometimes the thoughts will turn into visions. Some may be beautiful and others ugly. Treat them all with the same detachment. Observe them and let them go. Many will be of a psychic nature, such as prophecies or glimpses of things happening in other places. But, for the time being, let these go also. Focus on being the unattached watcher.

By separating yourself from your thinking, you attune yourself with what Western mystics call the "Overself" – the higher you. This extends into the afterlife and beyond. You may experience being the watcher of the watcher and come closer to a realization of the true nature of the Self.

The meditation exercises outlined here are a starting point for greater inner awareness. By opening the third-eye centre, you have taken the first serious steps to true clairvoyance. But it takes lots of patient practice. The more time you can devote to meditation, the greater will your insight be. In India the clairvoyant gifts are considered secondary to the spiritual insights. Quite right too. If more psychics focused on the spiritual nature of their gift, then some of the appalling standards I see could be eradicated.

Meditation exercises for modern life

I conclude this chapter by suggesting a few very practical meditative exercises that can help you with the stresses and strains of modern life. Again we use the power of visualization, which is the basis of clairvoyance. In the next chapter you'll learn how to use meditation for psychic purposes.

Before proceeding, prove to yourself the power of the imagination. Picture yourself holding half a lemon. Imagine its texture as you hold it in your hand. Now imagine its clean fresh smell. Holding the picture in your mind's eye, imagine taking a great big bite. You want to wince because of its sharpness. If you visualized this properly, your mouth will now be full of saliva. You have influenced your body's functions by the power of your imagination. The same technique can alter other psychological and physical processes.

The energizer
This exercise is an instant detenser that revitalizes your energy.

See your body as being made up of billions of cells. Now imagine that they are being crushed together and your whole body is being squeezed into a golf ball of tightly packed cells. The ball is incredibly dense and heavy with no space between the cells at all.

As soon as the oppression feels unbearable, let the cells expand again. There is room to move. The ball of cells expands and fits again to the shape of your body. See the cells as full of light and dancing with energy. A rhythmic dance of energy fills your whole body and you feel blissfully alive – radiant with energy.

The worry cracker

Imagine that you are walking in a clear, cool mountain stream. The sky is blue and birds are singing. On either side of you are blossoming trees and banks of coloured flowers. See their colours, smell their perfume. As you walk upstream you come to a high mountain waterfall. You stand under its clear, cool, cascading waters. The waters turn to coloured liquid light and pour over your body and through it as well. As the many incandescent, healing colours flood through you, they wash away your troubles. There is no more worry, tiredness and stress. All is washed away in the living waters.

Colour has many healing qualities. Focus on their luminosity and you will be restored.

Instant sleep

Insomnia is awful – the more you try to sleep the harder it is. Next time you can't sleep, try this. Recall the times in your past when you were so tired that you ached to sleep. Perhaps you once did a night shift, or you studied late for an exam, or your dinner party guests just didn't take the hint. At some time in your life you must have been desperately tired. Picture these occasions as clearly as you can and you'll soon be snoring away.

If all else fails and you're still adding up the bills or worrying about people, block the thoughts with a mundane meaningless word. Repeat a word like "the" over and over. You'll block the thinking process and bore yourself to sleep.

Meditate and lose weight

Giving anything up is never easy. But you can have self-control if you put the power of your will behind your thoughts. The centre of the will lies within the third-eye centre. Open it as you did in meditation (page 32) and visualize an indigo light in the centre of your forehead. Now build a mental picture of yourself as you would like to be: slim. Imagine what it feels like to be slim. Imagine enjoying low-fat foods and feeling sick of stodgy junk food. Hear your friends praising you.

Picture the type of food you want to eat and see the rewards it will bring. See yourself thin — unearth an old picture of yourself before you became overweight. Imagine the feel of your sleek, taut skin. Taste the fresh food of your new diet and smell the odour of the new healthy foods you will enjoy.

Now reinforce the visualization with words. Make a promise to yourself. "By the invincible power of my spiritual self, I command myself to be slim. Nothing can stop me achieving my aim. I banish excess fat."

Repeat the meditation exercise as many times as you can during your diet. In moments of weakness, when the cream buns tempt you, use active imagination to stop yourself. Visualize that the cream is sour or that the bun has been used to wipe the floor. Think of something really disgusting then imagine again how joyful it would be to be slim.

This technique will not only programme your subconscious but also will penetrate to the areas of your brain that control weight gain. Active imagination is a powerful tool of self-transformation.

The same technique can be used to banish smoking, anger, alcoholism or any addiction that inhibits spiritual growth.

STRANGE PSYCHIC STORIES OF THE STARS

John Lennon

If anyone made meditation fashionable, it was the Beatles when they visited Maharishi Yogi in India in the 1960s. John Lennon took more than a passing interest in spiritual subjects, and it may have triggered his own clairvoyant abilities. He once said, "Spiritualism should interest everyone." John attended many seances during his life — an interest still continued by his widow, Yoko, who practises the teachings of psychic Edgar Cayce.

It is believed that John had a premonition that he would be shot. He even stated that his fear of murder caused the Beatles to break up.

"We were not bored," he said, "and certainly did not run out of songs. I was paranoid about somebody trying to bump us off." When he heard that the Beatles' former road manager had been shot dead by Los Angeles police, he said over and over again, "I'm next, I know it."

But John believed firmly in an afterlife. "I am an optimist about eternity. I believe in life after death. I believe that death is not an end but a beginning."

(P N 2 / 1 / 8 8)

Chapter 3

Auras

How did man communicate before the invention of language?

Nobody knows for certain. Our grunting ancestors would have been very conscious of facial expressions and body language. These, no doubt, played an important role in communication. (It could be argued that psychics mistake subtle facial movements for psychological triggers that they unconsciously read when giving a sitting. You can disprove this for yourself when, much later in this book, we attempt blindfolded clairvoyance.)

I argue that archaic man was also aware of atmosphere: the good and bad atmospheres of places and the atmospheres of people. The human atmosphere, the collection of electromagnetic energies surrounding the human body in an oval-shaped field, is called the aura. All living things have this auric light, which can be seen or sensed by some psychics. Its colours and brightness tell us about the vitality, health and emotional state of a person. Thoughts and memories are all contained in its field, and through the aura telepathy takes place. Primitive man may have communicated thoughts through the aura. Man's ability to perceive the aura has been temporarily lost but this is being rediscovered.

This chapter will show you how to trigger these long perceptions and use the aura's power for healing and psychic awareness. I've noticed that people I've taught have seen their psychic abilities greatly increase once they've understood how easy it is to see the aura.

Photographic evidence

In 1939 the Russian scientist Professor Semyon Kirlian made a scientific breakthrough that has, for many of us, "proved" the existence of the aura. When he visited a hospital in Krasnodar in what was then the USSR, he watched a patient receiving treatment from a new high-frequency generator. He noticed that the glass electrodes that were used created sparks close to the patient's skin. Something was clearly being charged and he decided to try to photograph it.

Kirlian used two metal plates as electrodes with a sheet of photographic film between. Then he put his hand between them and switched on the current, releasing a high-voltage spark. When the film was developed it showed, to Kirlian's amazement, his hand surrounded by a bright glowing corona, which he named the "bioplasmic energy".

Other scientists were quick to discredit Kirlian's discovery. Professor Ellison argued that it was simply the effect of intermittent ionization of the air around the object being photographed, an effect known as "Lichtenberg figures".

But what the sceptics can't easily explain away is why a living leaf, when photographed, has a bright aura yet a dead one has a dull one. Also if part of a leaf is removed, the Kirlian photograph shows a ghost image of the missing segment. Furthermore, how can they explain the fact that healers' hands produce flare-like effects from the fingertips when they extend their powers or that the corona changes noticeably if a subject is photographed before and after drinking alcohol?

Some scientists believe only what they want to believe. I despair at their bigotry. Jane and I have both been able to see auras clearly since we were children. How can you deny something that you see with your own eyes?

Mistaken identity

There are two optical effects that are easily mistaken for the aura. You may notice, particularly if you've been in strong sunlight, that clear dots connected by thin lines float in front of your eyes. These are not plasmic flashes of pranic energy, as I've seen described by some ill-informed writers, but simply cellular debris floating in the eye. They are a purely physiological effect and nothing to do with auric sight.

Another optical effect that has been confused with auric vision is the after-image created when you stare at something for a long time. Try holding a sheet of fluorescent orange card in front of you at arm's length. Stare at it for five minutes in bright light. When you remove the card you'll see a green, ghostly square floating around the room. This is purely an optical effect that can also be caused to a lesser extent by staring at a person for a long time. Again it has nothing to do with perception of the aura.

How to sense the aura

Some beginners worry that the fact that they can't see the aura means they obviously have no psychic gift. Jane and I know many excellent mediums, healers and psychics who have never seen it with their eyes, yet they can give excellent evidence and psychic insight. Although they don't see the colours with their eyes, they sense the vibration of the aura.

You must have experienced this yourself. Have you ever visited a married couple's house and inadvertently interrupted a row? To avoid embarrassment, they put on sweet smiles, pretending that nothing has happened. It's like the pressure before a thunderstorm. The air is thick and oppressive. You "feel" the emotional atmosphere.

You are picking up the vibrations of the human atmosphere, the aura, all the time. Surround yourself with angry people and, even if no harsh words are spoken, you'll soon feel under emotional attack. Keep the company of depressed people and soon you too will feel gloomy. Atmospheres are contagious.

If you were able to see the aura with your eyes, you'd notice that the couple were probably radiating angry dark red colours or the sombre browns of depression. A sensible psychic would see nothing at all. They'd block the vibrations and try to be as untuned-in as possible.

We'll go into greater detail about reading the aura's vibration later.

How to see the aura

Soft or low light is the best condition in which to first see the aura. It also helps to be relaxed, so bed is the best place to try this next experiment.

1 Turn off the lights. You don't want to work in pitch-black conditions and in most cases the street lights filtering through the curtains will provide enough light. If not, leave the landing light on and close the bedroom door. The small amount of light seeping underneath the door frame should be enough to work with.

2 As you lie in bed, hold your hands straight out in front of you. Look gently at them, don't stare hard – you need to gaze rather than look. The aura rarely appears as a bright light, it is more like a gentle heat haze.

3 Try fixing your attention on your hands while focusing your eyes on the bedroom wall. The hands will appear out of focus but this will help you get the knack of the way to look.

4 Now very slowly bring the fingertips of each hand towards each other until they are very close but not touching. The aura will appear as fine lines of blue and red light between the finger tips. You can try the same again just using the index fingers of both hands.

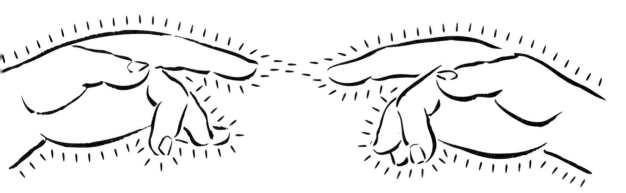

Watching the aura around the fingertips is a stepping stone to Auric second sight

5 As you draw the hands apart you will see the streams of energy connecting each finger. Imagine the energy increasing and you will see the light glow brightly. Bringing the fingers tantalizingly close together in this way seems to increase the auric flow. It's just like when you bring two opposite poles of magnets together: you feel the attraction suddenly increase as the fields unite.

How to read the aura

If you practise the above technique, you may soon start noticing the same effects around people's heads. The aura encircles the whole body like a luminous egg but it is brightest around the head. If you see dark or blotchy colours it indicates an ailment in that area. A dark cloud around the stomach region may indicate that the person suffers from a stomach complaint. If you see a similar black cloud around the person's head, it probably has a psychological meaning – they may, for example, be depressed. The aura is charged with their thought vibrations.

Bright colours have a more positive diagnosis. They indicate a happy, healthy disposition. The colours change all the time. Some people have a predominance of one colour but their moods and state of health make it change. You can look up the individual meanings of each colour in the list that follows but they are only a rough guideline. It is more important to trust your intuition. Tell the person what the colour means to you. What you see is only part of the art of aura-reading. The intuitive information you pick up is of far more value.

With practice you may see beyond the range of the visible spectrum and glimpse the ethereal colours of the spirit world. Consider the words of Sir Winston Churchill:

"I cannot pretend to be impartial about colours. I rejoice with the brilliant ones and am genuinely sorry for the poor brown ones. When I get to heaven I mean to spend a considerable time of the first million years in painting and so get to the bottom of the subject. But then I shall require a still gayer palette than I get here below. I expect orange and vermilion will be the darkest, dullest colours upon it, and beyond them will be a whole range of wonderful new colours which will delight the celestial eye."

Auric colours

Red

An aura that is predominantly red will indicate a high level of emotion or stress. "I saw red" is a phrase we use when we lose our temper. It is nature's warning colour, associated with the baser emotions of anger, hate, selfishness and lust. When tempers flare, the aura is seen as drenched in red light.

It is also the colour associated with the physical body — the colour of raw, earthly life force. Red is often present in the aura during convalescence from illness as renewed strength and energy return. Athletes too have a red auric dominance, mainly around the body. Ambitious and determined people like businessmen and politicians sometimes have circular balls of red light in the upper part of their aura, a sign that they have been focusing their willpower to achieve a goal.

A concentration of red light will indicate that energy is being sent to the nearest bodily area. If you see bright red light, for example, around the throat the person may be recovering from a bad cold. If it's a dark red or black cloud, they may still be suffering.

A pastel version of red, pink, is associated with the gentler feelings. If you see pink in the aura the person is sensitive and caring. It is very dominant during pregnancy — but does not necessarily mean the baby will be a girl.

Orange

Orange is a healing and cleansing colour. It has the vitality of red mixed with the optimism of yellow. Again it is a colour associated with recovery from illness or emotional trauma. It is linked with the spleen and the blood circulation and can indicate physical and mental vitality. Seen around the head, it shows a tolerant, open-minded individual.

It is also a colour of change: the subject may be planning a move of house or new lifestyle. They may be coming out of a period of inhibition and making a conscious break with the past. Balls of orange light around the head will indicate that they have their mind focused on changing their life but want to do so in a gentle way. And small flecks of the colour show that the changes have just started.

A concentration of colour around part of the body may show removal of toxins in this area. Dark muddy oranges show that the healing process is not yet complete, and if the coloration is close to brown the condition is severe. Muddy orange in the aura around the head may denote a lack of vitality or laziness. Brown colorations usually indicate an illness or depression but, in a generally bright aura, can mean that the person has an affinity with nature.

Pastel shades of orange indicate new spiritual aspirations. The person is seeking but has not yet found their true path. Orange is the colour of change and transformation. Counsellors, psychologists and social workers often have orange in their auras.

Yellow

Another colour of energy, yellow is associated with intellectual activities and self-expression. A person studying hard for exams will have a dominance of this colour. If the colours are pale and insipid, they will have to work harder to realize their intellectual goals.

Yellow is associated with the solar plexus. You will remember that in an earlier experiment we tried storing pranic energy here. Yellow is a source of spiritual energy and a colour associated by some with the psychic skills of psychometry.

Sometimes colours are seen in the aura as pin-like streaks radiating close to the body or head. If you see lots of yellow fine lines, it shows that the subject's mental activities are many and varied. Their mind may be split between too many things. They could be a worrier and you will feel a prickly, irritable sensation as you focus on their colours. Advise them to concentrate on one problem at a time and not to dissipate their power.

In emotional terms, yellow is an optimistic colour. In the tarot cards it appears on the happier cards. In the aura too it indicates happiness and optimism and is an indication of a cheerful, extrovert personality. Creative people often have a yellow auric dominance.

Green

Nature's colour of growth, green is the colour of renewal and is associated with recovery. Many healers have this regenerative colour in their auras. People with this colour also have a balancing and calming effect on others.

They are straightforward and loyal, wanting only the best for everyone.

Bright spring green will indicate someone who actively likes to help others, but if the colour is a sickly lemon colour it can indicate deceit or envy. But greens of nearly every hue are a positive sign. The rich emerald hues show strength of personality — a person who will give their word and keep it. The bright greens indicate a balanced person. Only the very dark black greens are negative, indicating an untrustworthy nature.

The heart is the focus of the aura's green light. The blood pressure and heart-felt feelings are linked with this colour. Associated with the centre of life it is the colour of harmony and balance.

Green is a mixture of yellow (associated with intellectual qualities) and blue (higher healing energies), and so, not surprisingly, many doctors have green in their aura. Also people who love nature — gardeners, ramblers, and horticulturists — often share the same auric coloration.

Blue

Associated with the throat psychic centre, blue is a highly spiritual colour. It is expansive, like the blue sky, and more than any other colour is the colour of healing. Blue calms and brings peace. It shows a love of freedom and a desire to reach the spiritual heights.

Mediums with the gift of clairaudience (the ability to hear spirit voices) have bright blues in their aura, as do writers, orators and talkative individuals. An aura dominated by bright blues indicates that the person is healthy and at peace. Visualizing cool blue calms the nerves and stabilizes fever.

Indigo and Violet

These are both spiritual colours. Indigo is associated with the third-eye centre, the centre of clairvoyance, and violet with the crown centre that connects us with the cosmic energy. Their

STRANGE PSYCHIC STORIES OF THE STARS

Shirley MacLaine

Few film fans are unaware of actress Shirley MacLaine's intense interest in psychic subjects — her books about it have become best sellers, and she is the leading light of the American New Age movement. One practical application of her interest is that Shirley overcame her fear of flying by visualization. Interviewed in 1987, she explained how visualization can help people overcame fear.

She used a visualization technique during a flight. "I decided to go through an experience where I would envisage what it would mean if I was in a plane crash. So I let it all happen to me, and I felt myself leave my body. The body took the crash, but the soul was left. Now that never really happened to me. I projected it so I could go through the fear and work it out." However, when she arrived at her destination, "The person who was meeting me said 'I had this terrible feeling that something happened to you in a plane crash.' Now that is mental telepathy: my friend picked that up through ESP.'

(PN 31/10/87)

presence in the aura indicates the integration of the higher nature. The spirituality of blue is combined with the energy of red, showing spiritual knowledge put into action. These colours are associated with the pituitary gland – the focus of understanding.

Indigo and violet are also signs of spiritual purity. I have noticed these colours to be present in people that devote a lot of time to meditation. They are the royal colours, the colours of the throne of consciousness. These colours are normally only found around the head. Vegetarians, however, who have considered the importance of bodily purity, sometimes have these colours surrounding the body as well.

The darker the colours, the deeper the person's spiritual quest. A predominance of deep purples can indicate a communication with the unconscious. Tune into these colours and you may be able to describe the person's dreams.

When violet is mixed with the purity of white to form lavender, it indicates that the person travels the highest of spiritual pathways – they have reached the mountaintop of understanding. Perhaps they should be giving *you* the reading!

Black and White

Although there is of course no such thing in nature as black light, the aura does sometimes show dark clouds that appear like a light. They represent the black clouds of depression. If black is a dominant colour then the person may be suffering with a neurosis or, worse still, be contemplating suicide. Use your counselling skills carefully and, if in doubt, suggest they seek professional psychiatric advice. If you know a good healer, or you have developed your own skills, suggest they have some healing.

Black clouds can also indicate tiredness and illness. If black muddies any of the aura's colours around the body, there may be a complaint in the area indicated. It may not be a serious condition but suggest that they get themselves checked out by their doctor.

White indicates the complete opposite of black. It is the colour of pure pranic energy – the life force. It usually occurs as pinpoints of flashing light and is a good sign, signifying health and vitality. During healing or mediumistic communication, white speckled lights are often seen around both the medium's and the sitter's heads. It means that spirit people and healing energy are present. In materialization circles, spirit lights appear as sparkling lights as if glitter dust has been thrown into the air through sunlight.

Silver and Gold

Silver is an exalted form of white and is the colour of the highest spiritual forces. It is the colour of the highest realms of spirit, the angelic kingdoms. When beings from the afterlife come to help, the silver lights are mirrored in the aura. Your sitter has God on their side.

Silver is also a colour of quick thinking, mental agility and, to a lesser extent, humour.

Gold is the spiritual protective colour. It shows spiritual strength, steadfastness and dependability. If you feel that a negative person is upsetting you, you can protect your sensitivity by imagining a golden light around the outer shell of your aura. This will stop you absorbing their bad vibrations. It's also a psychic self-defence technique I recommend to people who feel that they are troubled by an earthbound spirit entity.

How to draw the aura (auragrams)

Now that you know the meanings of the colours of the aura, you can give a reading based upon what you see and feel. Your sitter may soon forget what they've been told, particularly if it includes many colours and explanations, so aura readers have devised some simple visual aids to assist the reading. These are called auragrams.

The colour circle auragram

I   Draw a 12.5 cm (5 in) diameter circle on a piece of vellum paper, to symbolize the person's auric field. (Vellum or a lightly tinted paper is used so that we can include white.) The top half of the circle represents the aura seen around the head and the bottom half the aura of the body. Using coloured pencils we will draw the colours we see within this circle and explain to the sitter the meaning of each colour and their relation to the body and mind. Colours drawn close to the centre of the circle are those seen close to the body, and colours drawn near the circumference are those seen in the outer layers of the aura.

2   As your auric sight develops, you will notice that the aura has many layers, like an onion cut in half. About 1 cm ($\frac{1}{2}$ in) from the body is a red or blue light – the same as you saw when you did the exercise with your hands. This part of the aura is closely linked to physical health. If you see a bulge or noticeable break in this, it indicates a potential illness near the area. Flashes of white light are centres of healing energy.

3   Supposing you saw a shadow close to the left hip region and considered this to indicate a problem in this area. Colour it as a dark patch close to the centre of the circle at the 7 o'clock angle. Write a note of your observation outside the circle, but don't be alarmist. Say something like "Weakness in left hip area", and *not* "This person will lose a leg". It sounds silly but you'd be surprised how unthinking some untrained readers can be.

4   Next, colour in the rest of the physical aura radiating from the centre of the circle and note its strengths and weaknesses. Reds, blues, black and white are the most likely colours you will see near the body. Sometimes silver and gold are seen – an indication that the person is spiritually protected.

5   The aura close to the head should be interpreted in terms of vitality and emotional disposition. A black outline may indicate that the person is repressing feelings but a bright colour may show reserves of energy, or an inward-looking spirituality. The inner self and self-image can be seen in these areas. Draw these colours close to the centre of the upper semi-circle and again write a note at the side explaining your interpretation, such as "Yellow indicates that you are planning changes but some patchy dark colorations show that you find this decision hard and sometimes depressing."

6   At a distance of approximately 15 cm (6 in) to 23 cm (9 in) away from the head and body, lay the colours of the outer personality and

etheric duplicate body (the astral duplicate of the physical body). The aura colours around the head show the thoughts and personality that the person projects into the world. The ambitions and spiritual aspirations are centred above the crown centre at the top of the head and also around the third-eye centre in the middle of the forehead. The lights here can be seen as lazer-like lines of colour. In very psychic people they will appear like a peacock's feathers spreading in a brightly coloured fan.

7   The majority of auragrams have most of the coloration and interpretations drawn in the middle of the upper semi-circle. Use your "gut feeling" to interpret what these colours say about the goals of the enquirer. Again write some notes: "Your dominant indigo colours around the brow indicate a sincere spiritual quest, and the silver and golden colours extending above the top of your head show that you are expressing your spirituality in your actions."

8   Interpret all the colours here in terms of mental abilities and aspects of personality. If one colour is dominant, note this as the overall personality trait, for example, "An overall predominance of blue around your head indicates that you are generally calm and balanced but the flecks of red show that other people have been upsetting you over small matters." Again, use your intuition to decide what the colours mean for that person — there are no hard and fast rules.

9   The colours around the physical body are drawn into the bottom semi-circle. They can indicate health and a worldly nature. Draw in the colours and write a note such as, "Strong red surrounding most of your lower body shows that your passions dominant. You have a need to express yourself physically."

Jayne Mansfield

Jayne Mansfield's hairdresser was a medium and they used to hold seances in the home of Houdini's widow. Jayne Mansfield received some excellent spirit proof: "The woman I admired most, Ethel Barrymore," Jayne said, "spoke to me. Then my Aunt Kathy, who had been dead these 15 years, talked to me and her voice was exactly as I remembered it. Aunt Kathy always had a great sense of humour. She still had." Jayne also held seances in Valentino's former home, Falcon Lair, and received guidance from the "dead" silent-screen legend.

10 The aura extends all around the body like a luminous egg. If a person is tired and run down, the aura will hug the body. The happier and more relaxed we feel, the more the aura expands. Spiritually evolved people have a bright, expansive aura that revitalizes the people they meet. Depressed individuals draw their energy from others, and you may find that they deplete your own auric energy. Some people, particularly worriers, have breaks in their aura that leak energy. If you see this, you can influence their aura by visualizing a patch of protective golden light extending from yourself and stopping the energy loss. Note the breaks in the aura on your auragram.

11 The outermost part of the aura is hardest to see but is very important. It shows the subject's higher spiritual nature. Vibrations and colours you sense here should be interpreted as the spiritual goals that the individual should climb towards. Draw them on the outer edges of your circle.

12 Lastly, there are energies entering the aura. These are called the "rays" and appear like beams of coloured searchlights. We draw these energies from the cosmic source that permeates all planes of existence. Guardian spirits from the higher realms of spirit are said to be the transmitters of this energy. Draw these colours so they extend outside the circumference of the circle. They are the healing colours that the person needs, for instance, a person with an angry red aura may have a white or blue ray that is trying to balance their emotions. Or a dark cloud of illness may have a white ray as healing energy is drawn to it. Sometimes these rays are seen as a series of coloured bars that run horizontally or vertically through the aura.

STRANGE PSYCHIC STORIES OF THE STARS

Englebert Humperdinck

When Englebert Humperdinck bought Jayne Mansfield's old Hollywood home shortly after her death he said, "I'm sure she lived with me in spirit for a time – I'd smell her rose petal perfume. Once I saw a figure in a long, black dress in front of me. It was Jayne, but it wasn't frightening."

(Hello 6/11/93)

The symbolic auragram

Not everyone sees with clarity the colours of the aura. Sometimes we feel only the vibrations and atmosphere of the person. But this is of even more importance than auric sight. The colours you draw can be "seen" using your intuitive insights. You may feel that a person has a red aura even though you don't actually see it with your eyes. The pictures coming into your mind's eye are picked up by telepathy as you link your own aura with the sitter's. In the early stages they may be symbolic but, as you progress, the information that you take in by intuition will become more specific. For example, you may see a picture of a house which could mean that the person loves the home or that they may be planning a move. Incorporate the images you see into your auragram and draw them as little cameo symbols around the edge of your sheet of paper. When you get really efficient, you may be able to give them the correct street number and address of where they live to add to your picture.

Some symbols may be less direct. For example, if you see a snake it could mean that the person is surrounded by jealousy. Draw the picture and include a bit of red light around your snake image to indicate that the image represents a negative vibration. Explain each picture to your sitter and work with them to unravel the symbolism as you would a dream.

Colour breathing

It's possible to influence the colours of the aura using the pranic energy drawn in through the breath. To do this, you can adapt the pranic breathing exercise that you were taught on page 28. You will remember how we visualized breathing in white light and breathing out dark toxic smoke. Try the same exercise but visualize breathing in coloured light.

Decide which colour it is you need most. I suggest that you avoid the earthly vibrations of red and, of course, never use the browns or black. Breathing in the spiritual and healing colours of blue, green or violet has a positive effect. You can't go far wrong with the protective colours of silver and gold, and yellow will stimulate your energy.

Psychic experiment

Visualizing the aura

Jane had gone to bed by the time I returned late one evening from a public demonstration of mediumship. She commented on how bright my aura was as I entered the darkened bedroom. (When you've been working mediumistically the aura expands and becomes drenched in light.) I was in a spiritual mood and Jane commented how my aura was a vivid blue. "Tell me which colour you see now," I said and proceeded to visualize my aura changing to a bright yellow. Jane got it right and said "yellow". Each time I visualized a different colour Jane would see it in my aura.

You can try this yourself. Ask your partner or a friend to visualize their aura as being drenched in a coloured light. Then tell them which colour they're thinking of. It's a remarkably accurate experiment to try and will considerably improve your auric sight.

The chakras

The aura has seven major focuses of energy, called chakras, that correspond to the endocrine glands of the body and run upwards along the spinal chord. They are the link between the physical and auric bodies.

The word chakra means "wheel" in Sanskrit. Some see them as a swirling vortex of light and others describe them as lotuses with varying numbers of petals. There are further, less important chakras, and Eastern and Western systems differ slightly but for our purpose we will concentrate on the seven major centres.

Figure 1 on page 53 shows the location of the seven major chakras on the physical body. Each chakra on the front of the body is paired with its counterpart on the spine; together they are considered the front and rear aspects of one chakra (Figure 2). The lower centres are linked with the body and the higher centre with spiritual qualities. Each has an auric colour and psychic function.

Base (colour red)
The seat of energy, the base centre is the source of our physical strength and vitality. It is located at the base of the spine and from it we draw the energy of the earth. It is the powerhouse that provides the cosmic energy to drive the other psychic centres.

Sacral (colour orange)
The Sacral centre refines and filters the cosmic energy. It has a healing function and links the astral body with the physical. Situated below the navel, it is the auric gate to out-of-body travel.

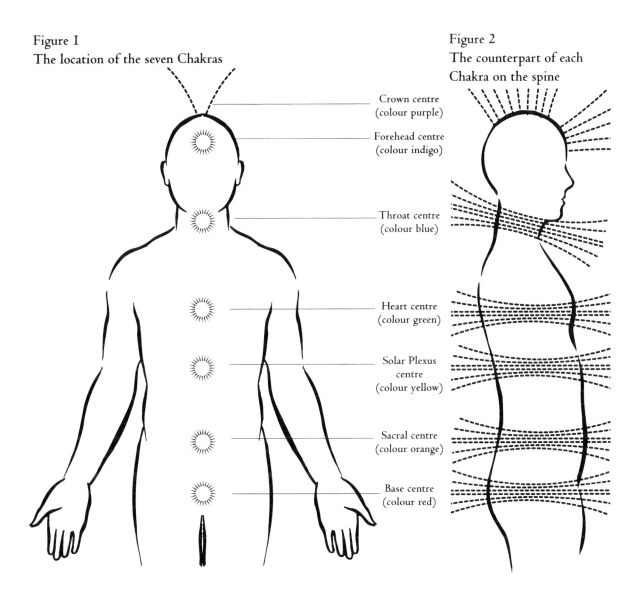

Figure 1
The location of the seven Chakras

Figure 2
The counterpart of each
Chakra on the spine

Crown centre
(colour purple)

Forehead centre
(colour indigo)

Throat centre
(colour blue)

Heart centre
(colour green)

Solar Plexus
centre
(colour yellow)

Sacral centre
(colour orange)

Base centre
(colour red)

Solar plexus (colour yellow)

Just below the rib cage is a network of nerves called the solar plexus. This chakra is our psychic battery. It is a sensitive centre that responds emotionally to impressions. It is used in psychometry to define the emotional nature of the information received.

Heart (colour green)

The highest of the emotional centres, the heart chakra is located in the centre of the chest. It has control of the three centres below it and converts instinct into feeling. Compassion, tolerance and sympathy are all governed by this centre. In psychic work it senses the love and presence of spirit people or the emotional state of the sitter. Its energy provides the impetus to spiritual development.

Throat (colour blue)

Situated at the top of the throat, this is the first of the three spiritual centres. It is the centre of creative abilities and verbal communication in this life and the next. It is the seat of clairaudience, and in physical mediumship ectoplasm builds over this centre to produce direct voice phenomena. In mental mediumship it is the source of the cosmic energy that enables mediums to hear the spirit voices. For psychic work it is the source of your own inner voice of intuition.

Forehead (colour indigo)

Known by most people as the "third-eye", the centre in the middle of the forehead is the seat of clairvoyance. It is here that we see pictures and imagery relating to the sitter and our own lives. It is closely interlinked with the throat and crown centre; together they work to provide our psychic insights. Self-confident and disciplined development of this centre results in visions and revelations that step beyond the realms of the imagination.

Crown (colour violet)

Although associated with the colour violet, this centre, known in the East as the "thousand-petalled lotus", is in fact a mixture of many brilliant colours like the feathers of a peacock fanning out from the top of the head. Our link with the infinite, the crown centre floods the aura with energy, wisdom and spiritual insight. It is through this centre that the soul leaves the physical body to take its place in the beyond. Nurses have described seeing twinkling lights above this centre when terminally ill patients die. The crown centre is the most spiritual of the charkras. Kundalini yoga describes how the 'coiled serpent' energy from the base centre rises along the spine to the crown. When the two energies unite, say the yogis, the adept attains God realization.

How to open the aura

All psychic abilities are linked to the aura. When we use our clairvoyant skills the aura expands as the psychic faculties are activated. If we can control the opening and closing of the aura at will, we control our psychic abilities. Consequently this next section is the most important stepping stone to psychic development. If you open the aura before any of the psychic experiments listed in this book, you will discover that your psychic abilities are greatly magnified. When you've mastered this skill thoroughly you can retry the experiments so far. You will find that your skills have taken a quantum leap.

The technique that follows is therefore the key to psychic awareness. By learning to open the aura by means of the chakras, we attune ourselves to the subtle vibrations coming to us from our sitters and people in the afterlife. You can use this technique before any of the psychic experiments described in this book.

A word of warning: it is quite safe to proceed with the following techniques if your motives are right and you set your heart and mind on the highest spiritual ideas. However, never open the aura and leave it open. It is very important to "close down" after you have finished. If you don't, you will pick up vibrations you may not want.

I learned this lesson the hard way. Having finished a clairvoyant session in London, I had to dash to catch the last train home. There was no time to "close down". And, just like in the famous comedy sketch, the crazy sat next to me on the tube. My opened aura picked up all his schizophrenic distress and I felt uncomfortable for days later. Now, I always "close down" — even if it means missing the train.

How to open

Sit quietly and meditate for a few minutes. You may want to calm yourself first by using one of the breathing techniques described in chapter 2. When you feel at peace with your thoughts, imagine sending out loving vibrations into the etheric. Ask that your invisible helpers from the world unseen draw close and protect you in your work. Some people prefer a simple prayer. Your sincerity of motive is an invincible protection — dark forces cannot penetrate the light.

I would suggest that you dictate the following instructions onto a cassette and play it during your meditation. Pause from time to time so that you don't have to rush to keep up with the tape. In time you'll learn this simple technique by heart, but even after years of practice I still inwardly talk myself through this technique to help me "open up".

1 Visualize that below you is a sea of white light. This is the nurturing, loving light of the earth. As you slowly breathe in, imagine drawing a bright ball of white light into the chakra at the base of the spine. As you do this, feel the activity in this centre. It opens like an incandescent flower and swirls and glows with red light.

2 Next, fix your attention again on the sea of light below you and pull another comet of white light up through the base centre and upwards to fill the sacral chakra below the navel. See it open like an orange flower. It is alive with energy and shines its orange rays outwards.

3 Return your awareness to the sea of light below you. Gather more energy and pull it upwards, through the base centre and through the sacral centre, and feel it illuminate the solar plexus with brilliant yellow light.

4 Each time you raise the energy through the centres, feel them fill with more and more energy. The more powerful your visualization, the more energy is drawn into the centres. You can use the inward breath to increase this flow but may pause from time to time between the opening of each chakra.

5 As you proceed you will feel your body becoming lighter. This is the sensation produced as the astral body becomes free of its physical prison. You may feel exhilarated and inspired – a sign that the spiritual energy is filling you.

6 Fix your attention again on the sea of light below you and pull even more light up through the base centre, through the sacral centre and through the solar plexus centre, and now fill the heart centre in the middle of the chest with light. The colour here is green. See green light opening like a flower with lazer beams shining from your aura. Feel the joy and emotion as you begin to attune yourself to your spiritual nature.

7   Return to the sea of light. Pull a great ball of light upwards again: through the base centre, through the sacral centre, through the solar plexus centre and through the heart centre, and now fill the centre at the top of the throat with radiant blue light. The lotus opens, and the throat centre is alive with vital energy. You will feel a slight irritation in this centre, a sign that it is fully open. Also imagine that the centre extends to the back of your head. Feel this too fill with light.

8   Again return to the sea of light below you. Gather huge quantities of energy and pull it up through the base centre, through the sacral centre, through the solar plexus, through the heart centre, through the throat centre and now fill the centre of the forehead with indigo light. As you do this, you may start to see through the third eye. Colours of many hues will appear gently glowing from the edges of your peripheral vision.

9   You are nearly finished. Return your consciousness to the sea of light below you and gather great quantities of light – it has a long way to travel. Now, draw the energy in through the base centre, through the sacral centre, through the solar plexus centre – feeling each centre overflowing with light – through the heart centre, through the throat centre, through the brow centre. And now feel the top of your head explode with brilliant rays of light. They extend high above you, touching the sky. You feel blissful and free. Beautiful ethereal colours shine from you. You radiate light. All your chakras are now open.

10 As a final step I now draw light directly from the source below to the crown centre. This time, focus on the sea of light below you and draw it through the base centre and upwards through the spine. There are three nerve channels, called Nadis. The energy travels through the central channel. Feel the light enter the base centre and move like a golden rod up the spine and radiate from the crown centre. As the light moves, see your spine as filled with light of many fibrous colours. You have now completed the first stages of opening your psychic awareness. Your aura is open and has expanded.

How to charge the aura with power

The next step is to cleanse and charge the aura. To do this we flush light from the opposite direction through the crown centre.

1 Once you've opened your centres as just described, visualize above you a great golden sun of light. This is the light of heaven, the great shining sun of God's energy.

2 Imagine its golden rays pouring down through your body and out of your fingertips and toes. It streams through you and as it does it washes away your stresses and strains. Your worries are washed away, your tiredness, your fears and doubts — all is washed clean by this vital loving light.

3 Now fill yourself with golden light. Feel the light filling you like liquid. It streams through the crown centre. It fills first your toes and feet. Fill your legs and trunk. Fill your hands and arms, your chest and head until you overflow like a chalice filled with liquid light.

4 Now let more energy stream down from above and fill your outer aura as well. See yourself as if enclosed in a gigantic egg of fibrous light. Fill this too with light. Feel the golden rays cling to your body and fill all of your aura.

Now what?

You will feel tremendously sensitive after you've finished the above — sensitive enough to feel the vibrations of other people's auras and the vibrations imprinted on objects that we will later learn to read with psychometry. If you look at your hands, you may see your own aura or you may see the auras around people's heads. The level of consciousness you have now entered is the basis of all psychic skills. For centuries it was the closely guarded secret knowledge of both yoga and Western mystical teachings.

You are now ready to test your psychic skills. Auras, psychometry, dowsing, tarot, tasseography, astral travel — all the skills I'll teach you can be increased a thousand-fold if you learn to master the foregoing technique.

Later I'll teach you how to use this "opening-up" technique to develop a communication with the afterlife — the first stages in mediumship.

A psychic's self-defence

I suggest that you record this next technique (How to close down — steps 1-6) on the other side of your cassette or directly after the recording you made of "How to open" so that it's to hand whenever you've finished working psychically. Speak into the recorder with a gentle reassuring tone. If you like, you could have some gentle music playing in the background.

Learning to close down after doing your psychic work is even more important than opening up in the first place. When I'm not working psychically I keep my centres firmly shut. If I tuned in to every vibration that came my way I'd soon be a gibbering wreck. Psychics that push their clairvoyance on you at every opportunity are normally not much good; they waste their energy. Close your aura after working and the power recharges ready for the next time you want to work.

As you become more proficient at opening, however, you will find that it is possible to open the chakras very quickly. Nevertheless, for the best results it is best to systematically go through the techniques I've outlined.

So, you've done your psychic work and now we're going to turn off the energy. Sit comfortably and quieten the breath. Closing the chakras is

STRANGE PSYCHIC STORIES OF THE STARS

Marlon Brando

In 1990 Marlon's son Christian was involved in an incident which resulted in a charge that he murdered Dag Drollet, the lover of Brando's daughter Cheyenne. The American press speculated that Brando's friends feared he came close to cracking "after he told them he was being haunted".

The actor is said to have spoken of sheets mysteriously flying off his bed and "cold ghostly lips" whispering, "I should not have died" in his car. The actor's former wife, Anna Kashfi, said he was convinced it was the ghost of Dag Drollet.

"It's terrifying," Brando is said to have admitted. "I know it's Dag's angry spirit."

Marlon Brando is no stranger to psychic experiences. He once put the famous Dutch psychic Peter Hurkos to the test by challenging him to tell him what lay in two sealed boxes. Of the first box Hurkos said, "I see a fire or an explosion on the sea. You have here a golden spike, a nail from a ship." Of the second box, Hurkos said, "And in this package you have a letter, and I'm sorry to tell you, sir, but the spelling is lousy."

Hurkos was right in both cases. The first box contained a golden spike from the ship HMS Bounty and the second contained a letter with misspelt words.

(18/890 PN)

done in the opposite way to opening but we leave the crown centre to last of all.

How to close down

1 First focus your attention on the brow centre. See the light get dimmer and darker. Imagine the flowers of the lotus closing and an iron door shutting over the centre. Light can neither get in or out. All is quiet.

2 Feel the light drop downwards through the throat centre. The light fades, the petals close and the door shuts. Now drop the light through the heart centre. The light fades, the petals close and the door shuts. Drop the light down through the solar plexus. The light fades, the petals close, the door shuts. Drop the light down through the spleen centre. The light fades, the petals close, the door shuts.

3 Finally, the base centre does not close completely. See the light here fade until it is just a small red light – like a chink of light through a partly opened door.

4 Now focus your attention on the crown centre that is still open. As before, let the golden light stream through the top of your head and out of your fingertips and toes. Give yourself a psychic shower. Wash away the problems and impressions that you've picked up from your sitter. They're not your worries. Wash them away.

5 Now fill the inside of your body with liquid golden light that pours in from the crown centre. Fill yourself up with golden light energy from the toes to the top of the head. Now close the crown centre. The light fades and the colours darken. I visualize two great iron hanger-doors closing over my head.

6 Quickly run through the centres again, making sure that all is quiet. Now, as a final safeguard, visualize wrapping a dark hooded cloak all over your body. Light can neither get in or out. All that shines from your aura is that small chink of light from the base chakra. Your aura has now closed. You are back to normal.

Chapter 4

Psychometry

Some people have referred to psychometry as "seeing through the fingers". It's all about reading vibrations left on objects by just holding them.

When you've become skilled at the exercises in this chapter, you'll be able to know the origin of an article, you'll know what's happened to it and, most importantly, you'll know about the character and life of its owner. Psychometric vibrations are left on all things — buildings, jewellery, watches, even plants and flowers. You are now going to learn how to sensitize yourself to these vibrations and give a reading. You may amaze yourself and friends as to just how accurate you can be. Next time you receive a letter you may understand its contents before opening it, or get the gist of the meaning of a letter even if it's written in a foreign language!

The atmosphere of place

Psychics believe that thought travels outside of the body and is absorbed by our environment. This would account for the sense of atmosphere that is felt in some buildings. For example, a church will feel peaceful and holy. Partly this is created by the cool air, the towering building and the coloured lights from the windows. But there is more to the atmosphere than this: there are the centuries of worship imprinted into the very structure of the building, which we describe as vibrations. The same applies to places with a less favourable history. A concentration camp such as Belsen has the opposite atmosphere: a dreadful "smell" of death.

Many of the leading archaeologists, such as Schiemann and Evans, have been attuned to this idea. Major historic discoveries are often found, not through systematic excavation but because of a hunch. Something leads the seeker to dig in a particular place and great treasures are unearthed.

The ancients were aware of this. We've all heard of the curse of Tutankhamen's tomb. Part of it is superstition, no doubt, but it's known that elaborate rituals were carried out in the Egyptian sites to project the pharaohs into the celestial afterlife. Also, it is known that curses were used to put off grave robbers — and even, perhaps, today's archaeologists.

These beliefs die hard. Uri Geller, the renowned psychic, has made a fortune in the employ of modern-day mining and oil companies. His dowsing skills have detected many new sources of mineral wealth. In some cases he would work high above the potential site, from an airplane.

Professor Charles Richet, a pioneer of psychical research, believed that these skills were a form of cryptesthesia — that is, it is the mind of the dowser that is responding to the stimuli. His theories raise interesting questions, particularly as to how maps can be dowsed to locate a site when the psychic may be miles away from the influence of the vibrations of the environment in question.

STRANGE PSYCHIC STORIES OF THE STARS

Catherine Cookson

Best-selling novelist Catherine Cookson, whose 72 books have sold over 60 million copies, revealed in her autobiography that she once attended a seance and was reunited with a friend that had committed suicide. "There is someone trying to find out who has lost a friend by his own hand," said the medium taking the seance. Pointing to Catherine, she continued, "He's standing behind you, and says you are not to worry any more about him; it was done on the spur of the moment." Adding that the communicator's name was John, the medium went on, "He is at peace now." Miss Cookson was astonished. A friend named John had shot himself two years earlier because of money problems. "His going had worried me for I had been near to following his example," admitted Catherine.

The startling revelations encouraged Catherine Cookson to delve deeper into the subject and she later befriended one of the world's greatest healers, Harry Edwards.

(PN 29/10/88)

Fields of energy

It has also been a long-held belief that certain places hold supra-normal powers. Divinities were associated with them: streams had naiads or water nymphs, woodlands had dryads or fairies, mountains had nymphs called oreads and the sea had its nereids. Some argue that the life forces of nature create fields of energy that amplify the vibration and atmosphere of place. There is a group in Scotland called The Findhorn Foundation who have harnessed these devas and transformed a previously barren terrain into a lush garden without the aid of fertilizers. They claim to have harnessed the natural spiritual forces of nature.

Dowsers insist that underground streams running under a house can seriously affect the health of some people. (Modern-day power pylons are said to have a similar ill effect.) The solution is often simple and may require a rearrangement of the bedroom so that the sleeper faces in a different direction, in line with a more beneficial flow of energy. In China practitioners of Fung Shui (a Cantonese phrase meaning "wind and water") are employed by big business to counter the ill effects of bad earth energies. One week after the world's most famous kung fu fighter suddenly died at the age of 32, a Hong Kong newspaper lead with the headline, "Did bad Fung Shui kill Bruce Lee?"

Earth energies

In the West these theories have been expanded to include the whole earth. James Lovelock coined the idea of Gaia — an idea that proposes that the collective properties of life are far greater than the sum total of its parts. Lovelock's ideas were a scientific approach to the ancient belief in Mother Earth. His mentors, including the ex-leader of the Green Party, David Icke, believe that the earth radiates a living energy, an aura. They believe that the earth is an organism with its own form of consciousness that guides the course of evolution, and that we share in Gaia's destiny.

A small but rapidly expanding group in the South of England endeavours to raise the level of vibration of the planet by consciously meditating on, and sending loving vibrations to, the earth itself. Jane and I have visited one group that visits places of power, such as ancient stones, to meditate and encourage these energies. The Fountain Group has now become a worldwide community-healing project. Originally it started from a small core of people who met by "accident" by a fountain in Brighton. Now it attracts hundreds of followers.

There is a worldwide network of similar groups who are beginning to interconnect and focus their energy. According to Barbara Carton of the *Washington Post*, there is a Spiritual Defence Initiative hard at work in the Pentagon, maintaining a "Peace Shield" around the planet. This is being visualized by the Pentagon Meditation Club. Among its members it boasts 15 Department of Defense employees, from civilian technicians to military officers, who gather every Friday at their "spiritual command post" inside the Pentagon.

The psychic time traveller

Objects that we own for a long time, just like buildings and places, absorb vibration. As the magnetic tape of a cassette recorder has imprinted on it music or words that can be played back many times, so also objects hold "recordings" of the character, emotions and memories of the owner. They contain the record of our lives, and a good psychic can tell from an object a detailed history of its owner. Sometimes this may include names of family members and friends, places that the owner once knew, and many facts about the person's past. This gift is known as psychometry.

Glimpses of history are sometimes a form of psychometry. The subjects inadvertently become aware of the atmosphere of the place and suddenly find themselves replaying in images events from the past. However, if our consciousness is not subject to the constraints of time, then it follows that they could indeed be seeing directly into history. Of course, the sceptic may argue that these visions are just daydreams and fantasy, but very often the person is able to recall facts that are completely unknown to them at the time.

Many psychical researchers believe that ghosts are an etheric record left behind by traumatic or repetitive events. I remember listening to a fascinating talk by the now deceased Gordon Higginson, whose mediumship was phenomenally accurate. He proposed that every event that has ever happened leaves a trace in the etheric. When we enter the spirit world we become etheric beings and would be able to relive everything that has ever happened by aligning ourselves with these vibrations. Consequently nothing is ever lost; all events good or bad have been written for all time into this great universal memory called the Akashic Record.

Improving accuracy

The impressions you receive when doing psychometry will at first come as a flood of mixed-up images. If you want to really impress with your psychometric skills, you have to unravel these and build them into a coherent story. Later, when you learn about the development of mediumship, you'll understand the great importance of getting your impressions into a well organized whole. The work you do now is the cornerstone of clear, concise and evidential clairvoyance that is the mark of a good psychic.

Students that sit in on my weekly psychic development classes are made to work hard, until their skills of psychometry are developed to an astonishing accuracy. Only after months of laborious practice do I let them progress to aura reading or mediumship. If you master the skills of psychometry, mediumship comes easily.

Psychometry is a useful indicator as to how much your accuracy improves. The percentage right will grow as your confidence increases. Later you can experiment with historic relics and describe life from long ago. Even the police have used psychometrists; clues as to a villain's identity have been unearthed when a murder weapon was held.

Psychometry teaches you to sense the atmosphere of place or read the history of an object. An extension of this gift is to sense the atmosphere of a person or become aware of people in the afterlife.

STRANGE PSYCHIC STORIES OF THE STARS

Robin Gibb

The Gibbs live in a centuries-old Oxfordshire house where once priests of the church trained to become bishops. The Bee Gees pop star's son, Robin-John, is said by his mother, Dwina Murphy-Gibb, to see the phantoms of their house's ex-inhabitants. The four-year-old boy described a "John and Mary who lived there and their friend Elizabeth. He had no framework for historical costume, but he told me Mary wore a dress down to her ankles. He also said one of the children had never grown up. I discovered a very detailed account of a John and Mary Rose who once lived on the site. They had two children, one of whom died in infancy." Dwina also explained that their son talked about a well, which was later found where he said.

She continued, "It appears to be a form of psychometry but he only needs to touch the walls and then he can tell you all about it.

(PN 14/8/93)

Improving psychometric accuracy

On page 23 you made a simple attempt at psychometry. Now let's develop this further. I've explained how to open the chakras in chapter 2, so sit comfortably and open all your centres this time (remembering, as always, to close down when you've finished your work). Take your friend's object as you did before and start talking about it. If you've been practising, you should by now be able to describe the character of the owner in some detail.

1 **The character** We need to structure the reading. First describe the character of the object's owner. Go into lots of detail and try to pick out any unusual character traits. Then describe what they look like. Are they male or female, big or small, old or young, fit or unhealthy? Try to see their features: look at their hair (its colour, whether they are balding, how long it is) and their eyes (the colour, shape). Perhaps they were deaf in one ear, or had false teeth, or had a limp. Dig deep with your impressions and build on your accuracy.

2 **The past** Next focus on their past: was it a happy childhood or full of

STRANGE PSYCHIC STORIES OF THE STARS

Tommy Steele

Tommy Steele, the famous star of stage and screen, was convinced of the afterlife from a young age. As a young boy he was taken ill and admitted to hospital. Around midnight, a boy came into the ward and threw a blue ball at him which the young Tommy threw back. When Tommy's mother heard the story she asked the doctor if they had another boy in the hospital with a little blue ball.

"No," the doctor replied, "but we had a small boy with a blue ball who died here two years ago."

Years later, Tommy Steele was taken seriously ill with spinal meningitis. As he lay in hospital, close to death, he heard a child's laughter. A brightly coloured ball bounced over the screens and landed just inches from his fingers. It took a strenuous effort, but Tommy managed to throw the ball back. The game continued until Tommy was able to get out of the bed to retrieve the ball.

The doctors couldn't believe how Tommy Steele had made such a remarkable recovery. "Give that little boy the credit," said Tommy, pointing to the bed behind the other side of the screen. The screens were taken away, revealing only sick men in the ward.

Tommy's parents asked what kind of ball it was. "Red with green and white stripes," replied Tommy. "It must have been Rodney," said his father. Rodney, Tommy's brother, had died a few years before, aged three. His favourite toy had been a red rubber ball with green and white stripes that Tommy had given to him on his last Christmas.

difficulty? What were their parents, brothers and sisters and friends like? Did the person do well at school? Perhaps you can describe the childhood home?

3 **The life history**   Gradually move forward in time. See their successes and failures, their hopes and ambitions. What were their emotional relationships like? Were they fulfilling, or was the person emotionally bruised? Did they marry – perhaps more than once? Do they like children? What work have they done? Were they ambitious or easygoing? You should ask yourself these questions and many more as you describe the story of the person's life.

4 **The present**   Keep going until you reach the present and then describe events that have recently happened: the car they drive, their home, work, friends, where they intend to go on holiday. The impressions you can pick up from psychometry are limitless, but structure your impressions and the sitter will understand you.

5 **Symbolism**   Some of the things they can't accept may have a symbolic importance. The psychic skills are very closely interlinked with dreaming. (The symbolism of dreaming is covered in Chapter 9.) Supposing you saw a raging fire but the person cannot accept this. Reassure them that this is not a prophesy: it may indicate that they have a flaming temper or that they've been emotionally burnt. You saw their condition in a symbolic way, so interpret this as you would a dream.

Psychic experiment

Reading from a distance

It's possible to give a psychometry reading without actually touching the object. I wish I'd used this technique when Jane and I were asked to demonstrate psychometry on a TV programme called "Late Night Live". We couldn't understand why the presenter was wearing rubber gloves when she collected objects to be read from the audience. But we soon found out – one of the objects selected was a sticky glass eye which she dropped into my hand. Like the glass eye, there may be some objects you do not want to touch, such as police evidence, a valuable painting or a relic in a museum. But our objective here is to further increase our sensitivity.

Have someone place the object to be read on a table in front of you. Don't touch it with your hands but imagine touching it with your aura. Feel your light body reaching out and blending with the vibration of the object. I like to visualize a beam of light, from my third-eye centre and stomach region, projecting towards the object. Link in like this and then proceed with your psychic reading in the same way as if you were holding the object. If you like, you can cup your hands around it, but don't actually touch it.

This technique is quite difficult to master but it's excellent practice that will prepare you to psychically link with people, which is covered in Chapter 10.

Psychic experiment

Targeted psychometry

Another simple and intriguing experiment you can try involves picking up a message deliberately imprinted onto a stone or crystal.

1 Next time you're at the beach, put some pebbles into a bag with a spade. It's best not to touch them with your hands, as ideally the stones should have never been touched before by anyone. They are totally free of any vibrations or influences.

2 At home ask a friend to choose one of the pebbles from the bag and take it into another room. Your friend should sit quietly for about 20 minutes and visualize an image or an intense feeling. The pebble will pick up their vibration and record the image being transmitted.

3 Afterwards you can read the vibration of the object as you did before. You may sense anger, love, or even a scene or picture. Tell your friend what you saw and whether it conforms to the image that they were trying to imprint.

The language of flowers

Flowers have always been potent symbols of the soul. Their mandala shape, their living exuberance and their scent are like the ungraspable spirit. And they make an excellent focus for the psychic skill called claisentience, which is the ability to sense spirit presence.

Psychometry is normally conducted with objects that have been owned for a long time. A living flower, however, will quickly absorb our vibrations and be used immediately to give a reading.

It's best if the enquirer picks the flower from a garden, as flowers bought from the shops may have been handled by other people; but in my experience it seems to make little difference to the reading.

Psychic experiment

Flower reading

Why not try this experiment with a group of people? Invite a few sympathetic friends to a "psychic coffee afternoon". You could start by demonstrating a little psychometry then move on to flower reading. If you really want to have complete confidence in your gift, at some stage you should stand up and demonstrate in front of an audience. Flower reading is a great starting point.

Have a large bunch of assorted flowers ready. Explain what you're going to do and ask each person to select any flower that appeals to them and to hold it for five minutes while you leave the room to make the coffee. Also have some baggage labels ready so that before you return each person can label their flower with a number or mark. When you're called in, you'll have a selection of flowers to choose from but will not know which one belongs to whom.

STRANGE PSYCHIC STORIES OF THE STARS

Bob Hoskins

The actor Bob Hoskins is reported to have had a psychometric experience when he worked as a porter in London's Covent Garden. "I was down in the cellar at the time, when on the wall appeared a woman's face. She was wearing a nun's habit and reaching out to me with upwardly turned hands. She spoke but I couldn't tell what she said. Later I learned that Covent Garden was once called `Convent Garden' and was owned by the Benedictines of Westminster." (*Living with spirits,* Harlequin books)

Seeing the nun was said to be lucky, and from that day on Bob Hoskins never looked back, soon becoming the world-famous actor we know today. Was the phantom a conscious spirit or a psychic impression left in the vibrations at Covent Garden?

Now sit down and tune yourself in. If you're nervous, don't worry. Surprisingly, nerves don't block you; they seem to help. I tend to worry when I'm *not* nervous about working with an audience. Adrenalin strengthens the psychic powers.

1 Select a flower and hold it in both hands. Use the psychometry skills you've practised to describe the character of the flower's owner. Build up a detailed description of their personality but don't say whom you think it belongs to or even try to guess. This will only distract you badly if you're wrong. Just talk as if the person's a complete stranger to you.

Barbara Cartland

Dame Barbara Cartland is another novelist that had a phantom encounter. As a teenager she heard footsteps and breathing on the stairs of her Somerset home. A psychic told her that the ghost of a fair-haired girl haunted the house. Years later, this was confirmed: workmen uncovered the skeleton of a young woman with fair hair buried behind the hearthstone.

(Hello 6/11/93)

2 Now you're going to talk about the person's life history and spiritual ideals. For this we use the structure of the plant as our guide. As well as radiating the vibrations of the person, the flower's structure will tell you a great deal more. Random events take on a special significance when used in psychic work. The deal of tarot cards, the fall of coins, dice or rune stones, the markings in sand or smoke on a mirror — all are random events. When the enquirer selected their flower, it synchronized with their destiny, which can now be read by you.

3 **The stem**   Look carefully at the stem, starting with the base. This represents birth. If it's damaged, this indicates a difficult birth or sickly early life. But don't just describe what your eyes see. Use it as a clue and "feel" more detail. Perhaps you can name the early ailment: was it to do with the lungs, stomach, heart, liver? The stem of the flower and its branches represent the person's life. Divide it into three from the base: childhood, mid-life and present day.

4 **The branches and leaves** Interpret the structure in your own way and continue to draw on the psychometry feel from the flower. A broken branch may indicate a failed job or marriage. Leaves that hug the stem could indicate a need for security, a close-knit family or an over-protective mother. Bumps and dark marks on the stem may indicate a difficulty at this time in life, and unopened buds may represent

ambitions, feelings or potentials that were never fulfilled. Blotchy leaves could indicate a friend that was ill, or someone that let them down. A stem that splits may indicate that they branched into more than one career or changed their life's direction. Talk about the things you see and feel and use the divisions of the flower to fit them to a time sequence. There are no hard-and-fast rules: use your intuition and the correct facts will come to you.

5 **The flower** Now you must turn to the flower itself. This represents the person's spiritual, emotional and intellectual aspirations and achievements. If most of the flowers are closed, the person may not express their real feelings or they may have a great deal of potential that they are just not using. Very long or damaged stamens can show sexual problems or a passionate nature. One large flower surrounded by many small ones can indicate they are surrounded by children or friends. Pay attention to the colours chosen. What do they tell you? Pink may indicate sensitivity, red passion, blue spiritual, yellow expressive, orange healing. The many hues will indicate the person's emotional disposition.

6 Look very carefully at every little detail. The centre of the bloom expresses the person's innermost nature. What do you see and feel? Peace and harmony, or is there damage here? Do the innermost shapes hug and protect the centre or do they radiate outward into the world? An explosive flower may indicate an extrovert character, while a fine delicate leaf may mean that they are sensitive or artistic. Damaged blooms may indicate family rifts, broken marriages or emotional breakdown. Flowers that stand high above the rest with a long straight stem show high-reaching ambition or spiritual aspirations. There are millions of different variations of form — you must interpret them in your own way following what your intuition tells you at the time of the reading.

7 When you've finished, ask whose flower it is and ask them to tell everyone how much you got right, particularly the fine details you identified with your psychometry.

Chapter 5

Dowsing

With a little practice, nearly everyone can learn to dowse. It is a visual way to recognise our response to psychic vibrations,

Dowsing is best known as a means of finding underground sources of water. But the art can also include finding oil, minerals, hidden objects, pipes and archaeological sites. It was even used in the Vietnam War by engineers to locate booby traps and underground bunkers. It has saved lives.

The origins of dowsing are not known for certain. Although written records indicate that it was first used by German miners in the 15th century, many believe that its roots go back much further. Certainly the ancients must have been aware of earth energies, and many dowsers notice that their pendulums and rods, when used at prehistoric sites such as Stonehenge, go wild. Prehistoric hill drawings such as the Long Man of Wilmington show men carrying two rods in either hand – a possible indication of a belief in dowsing skills. A cave painting found in the northern Sahara shows a man holding a forked stick, as do the carvings of the Peruvians, Egyptians and Chinese.

Learning to dowse is an extension of your skills of psychometry. Instead of tuning in to an object you'll tune in to a place. The same psychic skills that taught you to replay memories from objects can help you find a hidden object.

Dowsing rods

1 To make dowsing rods, cut a coat hanger with a pair of pliers as shown in the diagram. Bend them at right angles and place the short ends into a plastic sleeve — the casing of a ballpoint pen or two old cotton reels (spools) are excellent. Make sure that the metal rods can swing freely, and away you go.

2 To use the rods, you first have to decide what it is you want to find. As I've said before, it's the power of the imagination that directs psychic energy. Visualize what you want to find: water, cables, minerals or a historic site. For this experiment ask a friend to hide or bury something in your garden — visualize this object before you start. Imagine it as

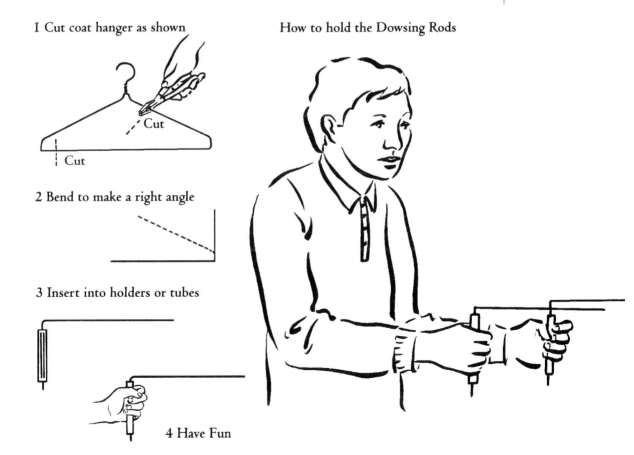

1 Cut coat hanger as shown

Cut

Cut

2 Bend to make a right angle

3 Insert into holders or tubes

4 Have Fun

How to hold the Dowsing Rods

73

clearly as you can in your third-eye centre at the middle of your forehead. Visualize what it looks like, its texture and weight. Some dowsers carry a sample of the target object, such as a bottle of water or a piece of a mineral or metal.

3 Hold your dowsing rods gently in both hands and keep your elbows bent and tucked in at the ribs – you'll look a little like John Wayne with his pistols. Systematically walk around your garden until the rods noticeably move. (There are several different types of dowsing reaction. The locator wires may swing together or apart or both may swing in the same direction. A few dowsers experience a pull upwards or downwards. The rods' reactions are different for every individual). Place a peg in the spot.

4 Walk over the ground again and see if the rods' reactions are consistent. If they are, dig the ground at your marker and you should find the "lost" item. Simple, isn't it?

Dowsing large areas

If you're dowsing a large area such as a field it would take hours to walk systematically all over it, so a dowsing shorthand is used.

First you need to decide what to find. If you decide to look for an underground stream, pipe or cable, the method is the same, only you'll need more pegs. Again visualize what it is you want to find – water, for example.

Stand at the field's gate facing the centre of the field. Say aloud, "Is water in this direction?" Then face slightly to the left and do the same, and again to the right. So long as there's only one underground source, you should get only one reaction with your rods.

Walk in the direction indicated, stop after a few yards and try again. Follow the rods' instructions and this will lead you to the water course. If you've walked over the course, the rods will guide you to retrace your steps.

The rods will react every time you cross the water's underground course. Mark the point each time with a peg until you have either a straight or meandering line. You have now located and marked the underground stream, but you don't yet know how far below the surface it lies.

Locating depth

A simple method to locate depth was devised by the French Bishop of Grenoble, who dowsed in the 18th century. The so-called "Bishop's Rule" is as follows:

Take a few steps backwards from your marker peg and ask the rods "Is the water at this depth?". Keep stepping back in stages and asking until you get a clear reaction from the rods. The distance from your reaction point to the marker is the same as the number of feet that the water lies below the ground.

Dowsing earth energies

The academic archaeologist Tom C Lethbridge, who came to fame in the 1950s, has been called the "Einstein of radiesthesia" (pendulum dowsing). His interest focused on the standing stones, like Stonehenge, which can be found all over the world. He noticed that his pendulum reacted vigorously at these places. He believed that the stones somehow amplified the Earth's energies and Lethbridge spent much of his life theorizing and studying these strange powers.

Half a century earlier, in 1921, Alfred Watkins noticed that, as well as the criss-cross tracks and footpaths of the English countryside, there was a network of lines connecting up old churches, standing stones, hilltops and ancient mounds. There were far from random. His book, *The Old Straight Track* (1924), proposed that Neolithic man had built these roadways to connect all their religious sites. Watkins called them "ley lines"' after the Saxon word "ley" meaning a "cleared glade".

Dowsers like Lethbridge noticed that Watkins's ley lines were full of psychokinetic

Jack Lemmon

Superstition is rife in the theatre and so is the belief that some theatres are haunted. Hollywood star Jack Lemmon claimed that his dressing room at London's Haymarket Theatre is haunted. An apparition, he said, "has scared me to death. I've been in my dressing room alone with the windows shut – and three times the door has opened and slammed when there's nobody around. It's terrifying thinking somebody, or something is watching you." Jack thought, "somebody might be playing a practical joke on me, which is not a wise thing to do for a guy of my age."

Staff of the Haymarket believe that it is the ghost of former stage manager Buckstone that causes the problem.

energy caused perhaps by underground streams running under the sites but argued by many to be a field force of magnetic energy. The further discoveries, that the monuments had astrological significance and aligned with the stars – discoveries which are at last being taken seriously by historians have attracted dowsers to investigate them. And you can too.

A psychic picnic

We live a short drive from Britain's most famous ley. Starting from an ancient burial mound about 1600 metres (1 mile) to the north-north-east of Stonehenge, it runs through Stonehenge, Old Sarum, Salisbury Cathedral and the prehistoric construction at Clearbury Ring, finishing at the earthworks of Frankbury Camp. It's over 29 km (18 miles) in length.

Before visiting your local sites to experiment with your dowsing skills, it's interesting to first trace the leys on a 1:50 000 scale map. Look for an obvious prehistoric monument and place the centre edge of a clear perspex ruler on it. Now rotate it through a circle and, with beginner's luck, you will note a number of significant points in a straight line. These may include churches, cathedrals, tumuli, or earthworks. Ley lines are more like a corridor than a fine line, so those monuments that fall close to your ruler's edge must also be included as part of the ley.

Choose a sunny day, pack a picnic and visit the site that appeals to you the most. It's fascinating to see how your dowsing rods react to these places. To dowse for a ley line you simply use the same techniques as explained to find water. Take a walk around the site. Touch the stones or the earth and, using your psychometry skills, feel the ancient vibrations. You may see pictures and visions in your third-eye centre of long-forgotten scenes of times gone by. Touching the stones at Avebury ring at night was, for me, an exhilarating experience. I felt my crown centre tingle and for a short while sensed the overwhelming atmosphere and saw visions of this incredible part of history.

Focus your mind on the concept of ley lines and walk around the site with your rods. They will occasionally react and you can plot the course of the ley as you would an underground stream. If you decide to follow its route, you may discover power spots that aren't shown on the map. A friend of mine, when tracing a ley with his rods, discovered a small standing stone of about a metre (three feet) high hidden and overgrown in the woods. It wasn't marked on modern maps but we found it on much older ones. Not a great historic discovery, but the fact that it was found by dowsing must be significant.

Using a pendulum

Pendulums have been used for dowsing for thousands of years. They can be used for anything from looking for water or finding keys, to diagnosing an illness, answering questions or determining the sex of an unborn baby.

1   All you need is a weight on a short length of string or light chain. I like to use a quartz crystal but really anything will do. Allow about 15 cm (6 in) of string or light chain so that the pendulum can swing freely. Hold it over this book.

2   Now ask your pendulum, "Is this a copy of the Psychic Workbook?". It should begin to swing. The direction of the swing will determine your "Yes" movement. It may be in a clockwise or anti-clockwise circle or it may swing from side to side. If you are unsure, still the pendulum with your hand and try again until you are sure of your "Yes answer". The direction of the swing will be different for each user and may change every time you use it.

3   Repeat the procedure but this time ask, "Is this a cabbage?" The pendulum should swing in a different manner. This is your "No answer". You can now ask your pendulum "yes" and "no" questions.

Zener cards and pendulum

Shuffle the Zener cards that you cut out earlier. Place five cards face down on the table. Hold your pendulum over the first card and ask, "Is a circle printed on this card?" Note whether your pendulum gives a yes or no swing. Then do the same for the other symbols: the cross, square, star and wavy line. By a process of elimination you will identify the card's symbol. You may be able to identify each one correctly. Chance would give you only one correct – get above this and you're showing signs of clairvoyance.

Another variation is to hide an object under one of three identical cups and, using the same yes/no technique, locate it. If you get two "yes" answers, try the cups in question again. You may make a few mistakes at first but with perseverance you will discover that you achieve far higher odds at getting a right answer than by chance alone.

Success with these experiments raises some intriguing questions. The pendulum is not in this case reacting to psychometry vibrations but responding to your own abilities of clairvoyance.

Map dowsing with a pendulum

In February 1994 two British skiers from Aylesbury in Buckinghamshire were rescued from an icebound mountain in the Bavarian Alps. They owed their lives to 73-year-old dowser George Horak. (Psychic News 12/4/94)

Hearing on the radio that Steve Swindlehurst and Ian Middleton were missing, Horak decided to dowse a map to find them. Using only a wire held in his left hand, Horak suspended it over the map until it pointed over a particular reference. He then phoned the rescuers and pinpointed a remote 1200 metre (4000 ft) spot on the mountainside. The missing men were found exactly where he had said, huddled and desperate in the freezing conditions.

Any form of schematic drawing can be used for dowsing. From a circuit diagram you could identify an electrical fault, an architect's plan can be used to psychically survey a house or a photograph may reveal facts about a person. But we're going to work with a map.

I Our objective is to tell someone their address even though we don't know where they live. Ask the person to let you know on which page of a city street map they live but not the road. The street map will probably already be divided into grid squares with letters running along the top and numbers to the side. For maps that aren't, you'll have to draw a grid on it yourself.

2 Now hold your pendulum by the number one and ask, "Does the house lie in this horizontal line?" You will get a yes or no swing. Continue down the page taking each number in turn and asking the same question. Tick the one that gets the yes answer. If two answer yes, repeat the experiment until only one is identified.

3 Do exactly the same for the lettered grid, asking, "Does the house lie in this vertical line?" If, for example, you got a yes for line 4 and C, you know that the house lies in this square.

4 Hold your pendulum over the square identified. There may be a few roads in this section, so eliminate the roads one at a time. Ask, for example, "Is the house in Church Street?" If you get a no response, move on to the next one and so on until you've identified the correct road.

5 If you are feeling really ambitious, you can continue by asking, "Is the house an even number?" then "Is it between one and 200?" and "Is it between one and 90?". Continue until you get a yes response for the exact number.

6 If you get it wrong, ask your volunteer how close you came.

Don't be disappointed if some of the results you get with the pendulum are wrong. Clarity will only fully come once you've learned to stop your subconscious thought from interfering with your intuitive insights.

STRANGE PSYCHIC STORIES OF THE STARS

Gloria Swanson

"I accept the afterlife's reality," said the actress Gloria Swanson when interviewed by American broadcaster Bryce Bond. She also described how she once left her physical body and "went a few blocks away".

Gloria, who passed away in 1983, accepted the reality of spiritual healing. "I have seen healer Miss Kuhlman cure dozens of people of many different illnesses. I have seen little children become hysterical with joy when their mothers or fathers suddenly walked after years of being crippled."

(P N   2 7 / 2 / 8 8)

Chapter 6

Crystals

According to legend, quartz crystals originated in Atlantis, the rich and powerful island civilization that was believed by the ancient Greeks to have sunk into the sea.

Certainly crystals were used by the Aztecs and Incas. Many claim that crystals were the power source behind their innovations. According to Edgar Cayce, the famous American psychic, crystal generators drove the airplanes and submarines he believed Atlantis to have possessed

Atlantis was lost but perhaps not the civilization's knowledge. Before sinking beneath the waves, some inhabitants were said to have fled to other parts of the world, taking with them the spiritual traditions and the secrets of crystal energy. The pyramids in Egypt are believed by some to have been built utilizing this now forgotten knowledge. The enormous stone blocks used in their construction were said to have been levitated using crystal power. The now lost cap stone was allegedly made from quartz crystal, and the well-known ankh symbol may have originally contained crystals in the rounded hole. The Druids, North American Indians, Sumerians, Mayans and Chinese all retained a realization that quartz crystals were in some way magical. And the ancient Greeks used the stones to cauterize wounds.

Whatever your belief as to the origin of their use, crystals can work for you. They can relieve stress, heal your body, record your dreams and even increase your intelligence.

The legacy of Atlantis

Has Atlantis risen again? Many think it has, but not in the physical sense. No seaweed-clad city has risen from the depths. Nor has a great earthquake raised lost continents from the ocean floor. But the inhabitants of Atlantis are here with us now — or so say some New Agers. And you could be one of them!

The unprecedented reawakening of the ancient magical arts, say those who believe in reincarnation, is because many spiritually advanced beings from Atlantis are reincarnating ready for the turn of the millennium. Their lost wisdom, we are told, is about to be rediscovered. The legends tell of fabled golden tablets engraved with the laws of earthly paradise. Some believe these were not made of earthly gold but were symbolic of alchemical gold — an allegory for the perfection of the human spirit. The inhabitants of the lost continent imprinted their spiritual knowledge on the astral light, and crystals are our way to access this ethereal time capsule.

But did this lost paradise ever exist? There are few written records of Atlantis's history. The most tantalizing references are provided by the ancient-Greek philosopher Plato in his two dialogues with Solon (the *Timaeus* and the *Critias*). Solon had heard the tale when he visited the ancient Egyptian city of Saïs and discussed Greek legends and traditions with a priest of the goddess Neith.

Writing in the fourth century BC, Plato describes a pastoral land with cities of great grandeur centred around a magnificent silver and gold palace and temple built by Atlas and dedicated to the sea-god Poseidon. Plato envisaged this utopian society dominating the known world 9,200 years before his birth. "There was an island situated in front of the straits which you called the pillars of Heracles [Gibraltar]; the island was larger than Libya and Asia put together."

But luxury and power caused corruption in Atlantis society, who refused to worship the Greek gods. Plato tells us that Zeus, the king of the gods, decreed that Atlantis should perish. "There occurred violent earthquakes and floods," Plato wrote, and Atlantis, in a single cataclysmic day, "disappeared into the depths of the sea."

Arguments still rage as to whether Atlantis was an allegory for the corruption that was then affecting ancient Greece. Even Aristotle, one of Plato's students, claimed that the story was fabricated. But only the unexplored seas that lie beyond the Strait of Gibraltar can finally settle the controversy. Despite the efforts of historians such as Ignatius Loyola Donnelly, Charles-Etienne Brasseur and Augustus le Plongeon, or the reveries of authors like Jules Verne, whose heros in *Twenty Thousand Leagues under the Sea* explore the city's drowned remains, Atlantis remains to this day an unproven myth.

The existence of South American legends about lost continents (Lemuria and Mu) has added substance to the Atlantis myth, and the statues of Easter Island are thought by some to be part of the legacy of Atlantis. The most cogent historical theory holds that the stories of Atlantis relate to the sudden demise of the Minoan civilization in 1100 BC. When Sir Arthur Evans in 1900 unearthed in Crete the temple of Knossus (the Minoan capital) he proved that there had existed a previously unknown and influential civilization. Ancient Egyptian chroniclers knew about the Minoan civilization, and it was Solon's Egyptian sources on which Plato claimed to have based his evidence.

In 1883 the volcanic island of Krakatoa, near Java, erupted with such a ferocity that it could be heard 3000 kilometres (2000 miles) away, and the resulting tidal wave swept away 300 villages and killed 36 000 people in Java and Sumatra. Did a similar event once take place in the Mediterranean? This was the question asked by Greek historian Spyridon Marinatos in 1932. His geological research highlighted the Island of Thera (Santorini) which could, at the time of the Minoans, have exploded in a bang and tidal wave even bigger than Krakatoa's. On the crescent-shaped island he was later to find Minoan buildings that had been destroyed by a volcano. Atlantis? Perhaps - but

---

STRANGE PSYCHIC STORIES OF THE STARS

Arnold Palmer

World champion golfer Arnold Palmer has experienced an enhanced state of consciousness when playing competitively. He said that there was "something spiritual, almost spectral", about some games. "I'd liken it to a sense of reverie – not a dreamlike state, but the somehow insulated state of a great musician in a great performance". He played "with an internal sense of rightness – it is not merely mechanical, it is not only spiritual; it is something of both, on a different plane and a more remote one."

Quotes source: Trance by Brian Inglis, Grafton Books. 1989.

Plato's dates were different and he had clearly stated that Atlantis lay beyond the Pillars of Hercules, in the Atlantic.

Nevertheless, numerous worldwide legends like the biblical story of Noah, the Babylonian tale of Gilgamesh or the Hindu, Aztec, and Mayan myths encourage many psychics, poets and philosophers to believe that Atlantis was a fact. Madam Blavatsky, the founder of the Theosophical Society, and later Rudolf Steiner, who founded the spiritual movement of anthroposophy, and W Scott-Elliot made incredible claims about the spiritual and technological feats of the civilization of Atlantis. These included an advanced technology comparable to our own — even fast airships driven by a mysterious fuel, "vril".

It was the world-famous psychic Edgar Cayce who, with his trance utterances of the 1930s, has most influenced the mystical speculation about Atlantis. Known as "The Sleeping Prophet", Cayce would drift into a self-induced hypnotic trance and prescribe cures for illness, offer information about past lives and provide remarkable clairvoyant insights for people who visited him.

He also describes Atlantis as having a spiritually and technically advanced civilization in the West Indies. (Carib legends also talk of a sunken land formerly connected to their islands.) The inhabitants could generate electricity and power airplanes from a mysterious rock he calls firestone. It was the misuse of technology, claims Cayce, that brought about the civilization's destruction. He predicts that Atlantis will rise again from its watery grave at a time when "the house or tomb of records is opened". Perhaps his reference is to the new chamber recently discovered inside the pyramid of Cheops at Giza? We'll not have long to wait for the answer.

What are crystals?

The very same geophysical forces that destroyed Atlantis created crystals. Rock crystals are usually, but not always, forms of natural quartz. Over 30 million years ago, when the earth was still young, a volcanic mixture of molten silicate rock, steam and gases became magnetized while still in liquid form. As this magma cooled the atoms within grouped together in an symmetrical pattern to form quartz crystals. The regular neat order of the crystal we see extends to the very atoms of the material's structure.

Scientists identify this inner structure by noting how crystals reorganize light, x-rays and other forms of radiation to suit their own structural patterns. Similarly, psychics believe that crystals can also alter psychic vibrations.

Crystals are all around you. The planet itself is 85 per cent crystal as nearly all the rocks in the earth's crust are crystalline. The paper of this book contains crystals and you can see crystals in sugar, salt, and in the ice from the freezer.

From the first galena crystal radio sets to the silicon chip, crystals have revolutionized technology. A gas stove igniter utilizes a spark from a compressed crystal and a quartz watch keeps time because of the regular pulse of a crystal. Pain killers, vitamin pills, paint, cement, polarizing sunglasses, china clay, liquid crystal displays, transistors, photography — all these technologies, and many more depend on the properties of crystal. They have initiated our technical revolution and are now part of the New Age spiritual revolution.

Buying your crystals

The quartz family of crystals is a good starting point for your crystal collection but you will soon discover that there is a vast range of crystals, stones and gems to choose from. Most are comparatively cheap, though the top of the range include the multi-million pound Krupp diamond owned by Elizabeth Taylor.

You may have read about the claim of American psychic Luana Collins that Liz should have stayed away from diamonds; they were too powerful for Liz with her poor health. "They gave her back problems, made her obese, were the prime cause of her drinking problems and soured her marriages. She became involved with stones that were too intense."

Too much of a good thing for Liz it seems, but for us lesser folk crystals can aid our health, protect us from harm and become a good friend. Actress Size and price are of little importance. Jane and I know many professional crystallologists who consider their best stones are the smallest and least expensive. They say that you don't choose the crystal. It chooses you!

This was proved to us when we bought our first crystal. We were attracted to a beautiful amethyst crystal in a New Age shop. I'd noticed that a number of customers asked to buy it but were told that it was not for sale. When Jane and I made the same request the response was quite different. (This happened before we'd achieved TV fame.) "This crystal has been waiting for you for three years," said the proprietor. "It's found its rightful owners."

This wasn't a tacky sales ploy. In fact, the shop owner, without any prompting, dropped the price considerably, telling us that the high price tag was just to put people off. When we left she said, "Remember, even though you have bought the crystal, you don't own it. It's found you – you're just its keeper." Our amethyst stone has since played a prominent role in our TV psychic experiments and many thousands of viewers have focused their thoughts on it.

Unfortunately, not all New Age salesmen are as honest. It's possible to buy excellent crystals at "Psychic Fairs" – Jane and I organize some of these. But we've also been approached by some devious characters who clearly are out to make a fast buck. They don't get a look-in at our events. But watch out for those that try to put on massive price mark-ups and have no interest in the spiritual implications of their sales. New Age shops are far more reliable. They're usually set up by spiritually orientated people who put principles before profit.

Your skills of psychometry should by now have considerably improved, so use them when buying a crystal. You may feel a tingling in your hands or, in the case of very powerful stones, a tingling at the crown chakra at the top of the head. Feel its vibration in your hand, sense its power, ask yourself which one feels right and let the crystal choose you.

Donald Campbell

Donald Campbell, the former British car and speedboat racer, believed in life after death. He spoke on a number of occasions of feeling the presence of his dead father, Sir Malcolm Campbell, with him in the cockpit of his boats and rocket cars. As he sat in the cockpit of the *Bluebird* and prepared to achieve his 648 kph (403 mph) land-speed record on Lake Eyre salt flats, Australia, he saw his father's spirit. "He was crystal-clear and looked down at me with the half-smile on his face I knew so well," wrote Campbell.

Then he heard the spirit say, "Well, boy, now you know how I felt on the morning of September 2 at Utah in 1935" – the day when his father burst a tyre at over 480 kph (300 mph). His father's voice encouraged Donald Campbell. Like his father before him, Donald became holder of both the water- and land-speed records.

Some stones to try

Here are a few suggestions to get you started. Later we'll show you how to use them and tune in to their benefits.

Clear Quartz This one's a must. Clear quartz can be as perfectly clear as cut glass (as used in crystal balls) to milky white. Clear quartz is "male" and active and is said to release pent up emotions. Milky white quartz is "female" and receptive and stimulates intuition, reduces stress and opens spiritual awareness. Choose a crystal that is a mixture of the two properties for maximum flexibility.

Impurities refine the vibrations and result in different colours. Some of the most common forms include amethyst, which is a beautiful violet; pink rose quartz; rutilated quartz containing fine gold-coloured lines; and quartz containing dark rods of tourmaline.

Usually quartz has a six surfaced point at one end. The top is often clear changing to milky white towards the base. It is possible to obtain quartz crystals that have a point at both ends — these are said to aid memory.

A small stone mounted on a silver chain can be worn as a pendant. If worn over the heart, with its pointed tip facing downwards, it will help you deflect hostility and harmful tension. With the point facing upwards it will stimulate your energy and increase alertness and physical vitality.

Quartz receives, activates, contains, amplifies and transmits energy. It is a useful aid to meditation and is often used for focusing healing energies. It can be used as a pendulum to pinpoint vitamin deficiencies in a person and if pushed point upwards into the earth of a pot plant will encourage its growth.

Smoky Quartz This is similar in appearance to clear quartz but has black wispy streaks within it

Ravi Shankar

When India's top sitar musician had a glimpse of the past, he discovered that it was his own.

At the age of 2½, he started to ask his parents for toys that were in "the house where I lived before". At the age of six, Ravi began to tell his parents about a past life. He claimed that he was murdered by two relations who wanted to prevent him inheriting the family business. They decapitated him with a razor.

Lynn Picknett, a journalist, researched the claims and discovered that a six-year-old boy had been murdered at the address described, and in the way Ravi described, six months before his birth.

Picknett wrote, "The strangest coincidence of all was that Ravi was born with a birth mark around his neck that looked just like a razor slash."

(PN 5/1/91)

that look like rising smoke. Some have so much coloration that they become completely jet black.

This crystal is less of a healing aid but for centuries has been used as a goodluck charm or talisman. Its dark coloration is suggestive of the night and is used as a means to access the unconscious, enhance dreams or to help develop trance mediumship.

Amethyst Another must and very beautiful. Similar in shape to the clear quartz it is filled with a radiant violet colouring. To maintain its lustre it is important not to expose it to direct sunlight or its purple colour will fade. Again, it can be worn as a pendant and will keep you calm, balanced and healed. This is a spiritual stone and favoured by spiritual healers. It brings calm at times of grief and promotes deep, restful sleep. It is also said to strengthen the endocrinal and immune systems and cleanses the blood.

Rose Quartz This looks more like a nugget of pink, glassy marble. It is the calming stone that relieves stress and is said to cure headaches. It's the perfect stone to give to someone whose experiencing acute anxiety and is an aid to calm hyperactive children. Rose quartz heals on an emotional level.

Amber The golden orange of amber has been used by jewellers since time immemorial. It is said to be lucky if it contains the prehistoric remains of an insect It's not strictly a crystal, but is the fossilized resin from ancient trees and is said to "remember" the ancient days since its formation. It will help you develop your psychometry skills, aid memory and will cure absent-mindedness. It is also a good influence on the endocrine system, throat, chest, spleen and heart.

Azurite This deep blue stone is usually either ingrained within other rocks or has other green crystals growing alongside it. It normally looks like a stone that has had fine blue glitter dust embedded into its surface. It is a basic carbonate of copper. Recommended by the psychic Edgar Cayce, azurite is a powerful aid to psychic development and meditation. Legend has it that it was the general healing stone in Atlantis. It inspires creativity and body well-being. It aids the nervous system and helps the blood absorb oxygen.

Cleansing your crystal

So, you've chosen your crystal but first you have to clear any vibrations from it that it has picked up from all the customers who have handled it in the shop. Some psychics go through elaborate rituals, taking careful note of the astrological influences of the moon. But the simplest and easiest way to clear your crystal is to hold it under running water for about five minutes. A tap will do, but enthusiasts suggest that the purity of a running stream is better. The legendary Chalice Well at Glastonbury is a popular choice.

Now you have to dedicate your crystal to your chosen use. To do this you must first get in the right frame of mind. (You may like to light some incense and candles, lower the lights and put on some gentle music.) What you're about to do is psychometry in reverse. You will imprint a vibration on the crystal. It's best to dedicate individual crystals to specific tasks but if you feel you want to change a crystal's use you must recleanse it and start again.

Dedicating your crystal

1 Sit comfortably, quieten the breath and enter a quiet peaceful meditation. Now hold your crystal, point upwards in front of you, and project loving thoughts at it for a few minutes.

2 Touch your chakra at the third-eye centre and feel a flow of energy leaving your head and entering the stone.

3 Next, focus your thoughts on the use of the crystal. Visualize this as pictures. If, for example, it is to be used for healing, picture the crystal as full of loving light and see visions of it giving strength to those that need help. Build powerful positive pictures in your head and project them into the stone.

4 Say, in your own words, an affirmation for the work, such as "I dedicate this stone to healing. Through the invincible power of love it will heal the sick". Say the words, out loud or in your head, every time you use the crystal and its power will continue to build.

The basics of healing

Crystals focus and amplify our own latent powers. Healing energy (prana) is drawn through our etheric body from the universal life force. You may see this as God. (I visualize it as a great white light that extends infinitely in all directions above us, below in front, behind to the left and to the right.) You stand before the greatest power in the universe. Let your heart become humble and feel its immeasurable loving grace. You are not the healer; healing flows through you.

1 To begin your healing work, first dedicate your crystal in the way just described. (The choice of crystal is up to you but most crystal healers use clear quartz or amethyst.) Now focus and still your thoughts and open your psychic centres as you did on page 56. Try to become aware of your aura and others' – this is pure healing energy.

2 Once your psychic centres are open, visualize a great sun of light above you and feel its light pouring through the crown centre and out of your fingertips and toes. See all your own impurities being washed away in this loving stream of light.

3 Next, channel the energy just through your hands – you may, if you've developed your auric sight, see many colours pouring from your fingertips. As you progress and your spirituality increases, you may feel behind you angelic beings of light helping with the work.

4 When you've finished working, cleanse yourself with light and close yourself down in the way described on page 60.

In the exercises that follow we will use the crystal as the focus for our energy. As you progress, you may decide that you are advanced enough to

STRANGE PSYCHIC STORIES OF THE STARS

Donald Sinden

Donald Sinden was appearing at the Haymarket in a play with Sir Ralph Richardson. Just before Donald's curtain call a colleague knocked on his door to collect him.

"We went down beyond Sir Ralph's dressing room and passed him on the stairs dressed up in his period costume. We said good evening but he was obviously wrapped up in his thoughts and did not reply."

At the bottom of the stairs they saw the real Ralph Richardson on stage. They raced back upstairs but the figure had gone. They had seen the ghost of Buckstone who managed the theatre in the 1860s.

Donald Sinden said of the encounter, "That experience certainly made me openminded about psychic happenings."

dispense with the crystal altogether and use only your hands held about 5 cm (2 in) from the subject. If you want to take your gift further, contact the National Federation of Spiritual Healers, whose address is shown at the back of this book. They will advise you and supply a code of conduct. I strongly suggest you write to them before working with people.

Important guidelines for healing

❖ Never advise a subject to give up medication or to stop taking his doctor's advice. If the patient has not seen a doctor advise him to do so.

❖ Do not make a medical diagnosis, recommend drugs or sell herbs.

❖ Don't push your services on people – wait until you are asked.

❖ Don't give clairvoyant readings as you work.

❖ Keep any information about the subject's illness in strictest confidence.

❖ Don't charge for your services.

❖ Most importantly, remember that healing is a *complementary* therapy *not* an alternative one.

For the purposes of our experiments I advise that you restrict yourself to minor ailments such as colds or aches and pains. Only work with people you know well. Tell them that you're a novice. No harm can come to them but make no promises of miracle cures. Conditions such as mild depression or a lack of vitality are also alright to work with. If you find a real gift developing, then get the right advice from the National Federation of Spiritual Healers (see back of book) so that you get detailed guidance and stay within the law.

Healing plants

(clear quartz, rose quartz or amethyst)

Something I've noticed when Jane and I visit our many friends who are healers is that their houseplants and garden flowers bloom and grow profusely. Plants clearly respond to the vibrations of healing. We've sometimes taken an ailing plant to their "Plant Hospital" and had it returned a few weeks later in the peak of health.

For this experiment you'll need a sick, potted plant. If you don't have one yourself, ask a friend if you can borrow one .

1 First dedicate your crystal: in this case we'll use either an amethyst, quartz or rose quartz.

2 Open your centres and feel the healing energy flow through your crown centre and out of your hands.

3 Hold your crystal and simply stroke the plant's leaves with its point. Visualize the healing energy passing from you, through the crystal and into the plant. All the time visualize the plant blooming and healthy.

4 Continue until you feel the energy subside, then stop. When you've finished, sit quietly and close your psychic centres in the way you were taught earlier.

5 Finally, place the crystal, point upwards, in the soil by the plant. The crystal will continue radiating healing energy like a cosmic battery. After a few crystal-healing sessions you will notice an improvement in the plant's health. (To stimulate the healing energy further, you could, like Prince Charles, play your plants music and talk to them.)

Another experiment you can try with plants can have immediate and startling results. Put some cress seeds in the palm of one hand and hold your crystal over them about 1 cm ($\frac{1}{2}$ in) away. Visualize the life force from your crystal filling the seeds with light. Examine them carefully after about 10 minutes — some may have begun to sprout!

Healing others

(clear quartz, amethyst or rose quartz)

You can work with animals or people just as you did with plants. Again, I stress that you should keep to common ailments unless you can receive proper in-depth training.

1 After opening your centres, let the healing energy pour from the top of your head and out of your hands. Use your quartz crystal as the focus and amplifier for this energy. Start at the subject's head and work down towards the feet, holding the crystal slightly away from the person's body. You may feel inclined to work more on a particular area — not necessarily the area of the complaint — and may feel drawn to the areas of the chakras.

2 The person's psychic centres may have opened as you worked, so before finishing imagine these closing. See a dark cloak wrapping the person, sealing their light and protecting them from external influences.

3 After the session wash your hands, cleanse yourself with light and close your own chakras.

Crystal-clear benefits

Here are some crystals that are considered to help particular illnesses:
Agate: tiredness; **amber:** blood cleanser and throat; **aquamarine:** eyes and liver; **aventurine:** headaches; **beryl:** liver; **bloodstone:** liver and iron deficiency; **carnelian:** kidneys, lungs and menstrual problems; **citrine:** gallbladder; **garnet:** sex drive; **jade:** emotions; **lapis lazuli:** epilepsy; **malachite:** asthma; **moonstone:** water retention; **peridot:** digestion; **quartz:** a general healer; **rose quartz:** peace of mind; **solalite:** blood-pressure; **sugalite:** heart and brain; **tiger eye:** inner fears and blood pressure; **tourmaline:** bad nerves; **turquoise:** strength; **varisite:** pregnancy; **zircon:** insomnia, depression and appetite.

Self-healing

(clear quartz or amethyst)

Doctors are beginning to appreciate the beneficial effects of visualization in helping to combat illness. Even cancerous tumours have sometimes been successfully shrunk using these techniques. The hypothesis is that imagination can create the same physiological changes in the body that real experiences can.

1 First cleanse and dedicate your crystal to healing. You may want to buy a specialist stone for your specific complaint but we're going to work with either clear quartz or amethyst – both are versatile and powerful healing crystals.

2 Lie down on a bed and place the crystal on your solar plexus centre just below the ribcage. Hold it there with your hands comfortably folded over it. Now visualize this centre opening and a healing light radiating from the crystal and filling your whole body with warm, loving light.

3 If you suffer from an illness in a particular place or organ, use your imagination to fill the affected area with healing light that radiates from your crystal. Reinforce this power by imagining that you are lying in a beautiful meadow on a summer's day. The birds are singing and the gentle sun's rays are passing through your body and washing away your illness. The light is cleansing you. Imagine the illness leaving your body like a dark smoke and being replaced with light. Breathe in light and breathe out the dark smoke.

4 Imagine the white blood cells of your body destroying the black illness. See the cells as an army dressed in white. There are millions of them, they are invincible and they are attacking and destroying the negative cells. You are feeling free and joyful.

5 Continue until you feel refreshed then just drift into a restful sleep.

STRANGE PSYCHIC STORIES OF THE STARS

Michael York

Michael York is a firm believer in ESP and takes an interest in the New Age movement that is spearheaded in the United States by actress Shirley Maclaine. He uses the power of crystals which are similar to the one we will be using as part of our experiment. He believes that a pocketful of them saved his life when six thugs attacked him and his wife in Rio de Janeiro earlier this year. The 50-year-old actor went to defend himself and to his amazement the muggers fled. He is convinced that the crystals, which were given to him by a Brazilian healer, protected him.

Crystal experiment 4

Dreams and restful sleep
(smoky quartz or amethyst)

To get a good night's sleep, simply dedicate a crystal to restful sleep and place it beside you or under your pillow. Amethyst, aquamarine, carnelian, chrysocolla, chrysoprase, flourite, jade, lapis lazuli, rhodochrosite, rhodonite, rose quartz, sodalite, tourmaline and turquoise are all good for this.

If you want to be more adventurous, some crystals can promote intense dreaming and even prophecy. Herkimer diamond will bring an awareness of dreams and calcite stimulates astral projection (leaving your body).

Amethyst makes an excellent dream stone. Hold the crystal to your throat centre, before going to sleep, and imagine it opening with a bright blue light. The throat centre connects to the brain stem which psychologists have identified as the area of the brain that controls dreaming. You should have vivid dreams that night. Chapter 9 explains all about using your dreams for self-growth and psychic insight.

Smoky quartz can be used in the same way but watch out: it's a very powerful stone and opens the dark recesses of the unconscious. It is said to help people who suffer from anger or despair, but you must be prepared to see yourself as you really are.

STRANGE PSYCHIC STORIES OF THE STARS

Edgar Mitchell

A former US Navy pilot, Edgar Mitchell was the sixth man to walk on the moon. On his return he announced, to the dismay of NASA, that he had conducted secret ESP experiments from outer space. Mitchell said of his moon experience, "It was an explosion of awareness, an 'Aha!' a 'Wow'. Instead of an intellectual search there was suddenly a very deep gut feeling that something was different." Unfortunately the experiments were not extensive enough to be considered an outright success, but they left Mitchell with a lifelong interest in the subject. He resigned as an astronaut only two years after his Apollo mission and founded the Institute of Noetic Sciences to study ESP and human consciousness. "There seems to be more to the universe than random, chaotic, purposeless movement of a collection of molecular particles." said Mitchell, "On the return trip, gazing through 240 000 miles of space towards the planet from which I had come, I suddenly experienced the universe as intelligent, loving, harmonious."

(The Mail, 17/7/94)

Study and memory

(amber or clear quartz)

Certain crystals are said to help you remember. If you're preparing for exams or embarking on a course of study, dedicate a crystal to improve your memory. Clear quartz can be used although many people prefer amber which is not a stone but the fossilized resin of prehistoric trees. It not only remembers the past centuries but also helps with absent-mindedness.

Keep your crystal with you as you study. Hold it while you try to commit facts to memory or when you do your revision. Put it under your pillow when you sleep and, most importantly, wear it when you go into your exam! Psychometrize the stone when you need an answer and the correct facts will flood into your mind.

The Akashic record

It takes thousands of years for the light from the stars to reach earth. When we look up at the night sky we are actually witnessing cosmic events from the time of Christ. If we could view the earth from one of the stars, we would see its history unfolding. And, if our telescope was powerful enough, we could watch the rise and fall of Rome, the Crusades, the First and Second World Wars — in fact everything that's ever happened to our planet.

Edwin Hubble's observation in 1929 that the galaxies were hurtling away from each other heralded the Big Bang theory — that the universe started with a massive, titanic explosion. With radio telescopes, scientists can listen to the microwave background radiation that is the echo of the beginning of existence, 15 billion years ago.

Psychics subscribe to a similar theory. Just as an object has a record of its history that we can access with psychometry, so too there is a record of all historic events imprinted on the ether. This cosmic record they call the Akashic Record. It extends into both the past and the future.

Crystal experiment 6

Unlocking the Akashic Record

(azurite or clear quartz)

The mystic Edgar Cayce saw azurite as one of the keys to unlocking the Akashic Record and the blueprint of history to come. We can share in these visions.

1 Dedicate a crystal to opening the Akashic Record – you could use a clear quartz or work with azurite. Sit in deep meditation and open your centres.

2 Hold your crystal in your hand and use your skills of psychometry to link into its history. But this time instead of trying to sense the history of its owner, tune into the history of the planet.

3 Let your thoughts free-associate. Just watch them, rather than trying to grasp them. You need to enter a hypnagogic state of awareness – the same flow of imagery that occurs when you are beginning to fall off to sleep. Now hold your crystal at your third-eye centre in the middle of your forehead. The imagery will intensify.

4 When you've finished your meditation, write down whichever pictures you can remember. It won't be easy as they flash so quickly before your mind's eye. As the Akashic Record also extends into the future, in subsequent experiments you could try looking forward in time.

5 When you've finished close your centres down in the usual way.

Of course, there's a possibility with this type of experiment that your own fantasies may take over. So, to prove your insights I suggest that you at first focus on a period of history that is obscure and that you know nothing about. Try something like the history of Japan, Afganistan or Nigeria, subjects that you are unlikely to have studied at school. Note your findings, write them down and check out how your facts compare with the books at the public library.

Chapter 7

Fortune Telling

"Anything done at a particular moment in time has the qualities of that moment in time" said the analytical psychologist Carl Jung. By interpreting random events we can know the future.

W e really stuck our necks out when Jane and I accepted the contract to predict "Next week's news today!" for the Big Breakfast. We soon realized that Channel 4's ground-breaking early morning programme was far from sympathetic to psychics. What they expected was a couple of whacky individuals that could bounce off the presenters Chris Evans, Gabby Rossiter and Paula Yates. If we got it right, fine. If not — well, it was still good television.

Focusing on world events

But they soon changed their tune. Chris Evans put us on the spot during the first programme transmitted. "So, you're going to tell us next week's news? You're going to make *specific* predictions with *no* vagueness?" We had to get it right or lose face in front of millions of viewers. But we did get it right. In fact the producer was so impressed that she introduced a scoreboard for our predictions: right, wrong and pending. Our success rate was about 85 per cent correct.

One week we made 13 correct predictions and there just wasn't room on the scoreboard to fit them all in.

As well as the news items mentioned in the Introduction to this book, some of our successes included the Queen being hit by an egg; haemophiliac blood contaminated in France; men walking to the South Pole; Elizabeth Taylor's heart attack; Rembrandt drawings found; a mock assassination attempt on Ross Perot; the French farmers' lamb protest; Cliff Richard losing his voice; a boy impaled on railings; Mafia boss Totto seized; footballer Paul Gascoigne getting a black eye; cult leader Koresh killing himself; Chris Patten having a heart attack; horse ripper attacks; oil tankers colliding off Indonesia; and an unscheduled meeting of the Queen with Boris Yeltsin.

So how did we do it? If you followed our spot you will realize that the events predicted were so unexpected that no scouring of the newspapers could have anticipated the events we forecast. And if it was pure luck, then Jane and I would have been better off concentrating our efforts on filling out pools coupons.

We used the psychic faculty of precognition. And it was exhausting work. We'd fax in our predictions the night before the show. Some, which were too sensitive or could get us into legal deep water, would be crossed off by the producer – which was a pity as these would often be the ones that would come up in a spectacular way. But we should have known this.

When you focus your psychic attention on world events, it's surprising how accurate you become. Sometimes the information would come to us when we least expected it – when we were distracted, asleep or day-dreaming – but for the most part we would meditate the night before and "see" the events.

Can you see the future?

It's surprising how many people can see the future. You can too – and probably already have. You just need to believe in your powers. The conscious knowledge that precognition exists is the most important step towards developing it.

Ask yourself these questions:

❖ Have you ever dreamed of a future event and it's happened?

❖ When visiting a strange place have you had a sense of déja vu – the feeling that you've been there before?

❖ Have you applied for a job and just known you're going to get it even though the odds were stacked against you?

❖ Have you known, despite their abilities, that some childhood friends would do well in life and others fail?

Sounds familiar? Let's now try predicting next week's news.

Tune in to the psychic news

Nostradamus (1503-1566), the greatest of all seers, used to focus his attention upon a bowl of water. He would see pictures projected from his mind and then relate the events to his knowledge of astrology. He predicted the Great Fire of London in 1666, the French Revolution, Napoleon's defeat at Waterloo, Hitler's rise to power and the nuclear bomb. But you don't need a crystal ball, water, a smoky glass or any of the paraphernalia of scryers. (Scrying is a means of practising clairvoyance or divination by gazing into a crystal ball although some scryers, use a bowl of water instead.) It can all be done inside your head. You just need an image to fix your attention on.

We found that the best time to work is late at night. The banal distractions of the day are out of the way and because you're tired, your everyday thinking doesn't get in the way. In fact, we discovered that the more exhausted we were, the more accurate were our predictions. The subconscious mind was more active the closer we were to sleep.

So, if you want to be a psychic newscaster, try this:

1 Sit in an upright chair, close your eyes and open your aura as you did on page 55. It's imperative that you do this and also fill yourself with as much auric light as possible. You are now in a state of extreme sensitivity and deeply relaxed.

2 Let your mind drift for a while but try hard not to fall asleep. You need to retain a state between sleeping and waking. Watch your thoughts but don't follow them. Be the observer of yourself. Instead of thinking in words, try to think in pictures. For example, you think, "I ought to do the gardening tomorrow." Convert this into a picture – see the garden, the flowers, the sky. Gradually you'll stimulate a flow of visual imagery. Many scenes and pictures will flash before your mind's eye.

3 Focus your attention on the centre of your forehead and see the visions concentrated in this area. Now imagine a blank newspaper in front of you with only the banner logo (the name of the paper) in position. Next transfer the stream of imagery onto the white pages. By linking the images you are encouraging your subconscious mind to associate the images it throws up with the future headlines. You trigger your precognition.

4 Then imagine the images changing to printed words. Try to read them. At first you may just pick up one or two words. You may only see "Prime Minister" but the next day you read "Prime Minister in sex scandal with naked nun". Also note the images. In the case quoted you may just have seen a picture of a politician holding a cross. Note what images you saw and how it relates to important world events.

The hardest part of this technique is remembering what you've seen. You enter a psychological state that's similar to a lucid dream and, just like a dream, the impressions can be infuriatingly difficult to recall. Also, many of the things you see may be in a symbolic form – allegories of future events. I keep a pen in my hand as I meditate, jolt myself out of my reverie and frantically scribble down my visions. Alternatively, you could leave a cassette on record and speak your comments but I find its low hiss a distraction.

Your first results may be disappointing, but keep trying – the more you believe in yourself, the closer you come to achieving empirical results. It takes time to learn to shift your centre of consciousness, but it is possible to do. Believe in yourself and focus on the future.

The paradox of time

Nobody understands what time really is. Even the scientists and philosophers are baffled. As you read this sentence it becomes a memory. Time endlessly passes. All we can be fairly sure of is that the present moment exists. Now is eternal. But what about the past and future? Do they have the same reality as this moment in time?

Time is a paradox. Eastern teachers who have achieved self-realization stress the importance of living in "the eternal Now". They are continually conscious of the highest levels of existence — levels that are beyond the mind and impossible to grasp with thinking. If we could comprehend the Now we would realize the meaning of the past and see the blueprint of the future.

I believe that a part of us remains in the past and a part exists in the future also. Our relationship to the past and future is determined by our present state of consciousness. If we feel blissfully happy, then the problems in our past seem insignificant. If we feel gloomy, our life history weighs heavily upon us and we feel that the burden of existence is intolerable. The past changes according to our state of mind. And so does the future. That's why I remain a hopeless optimist.

Only with self-realization do we free ourselves from time. If I comprehended the eternal now, I wouldn't give a hoot if I died tomorrow. I'd be spiritually free — living eternally in the bliss of the present.

But for most of us, spiritually grounded in the material world, it's not like that. We are bound to the flow of time. What will happen in the future is important to us.

STRANGE PSYCHIC STORIES OF THE STARS

Sir John Mills

It was as long ago as 1958 when Sir John Mills first publicly expressed an interest in spiritualism. And if he hadn't trusted his own intuition the public may never have heard of this great actor.

During the Second World War he decided to take his wife to the famous Café de Paris in London. For some inexplicable reason he changed his mind and insisted that they go for a walk in the park instead. That night proved to be one of the worst in the London Blitz. A bomb smashed through the nightclub Sir John and his wife had planned to visit, causing countless casualties.

Sir John's sister, Annette, also is interested in psychic things. Badly injured in a wartime car crash, she was saved from an invalid's life with healing from Nan Mackenzie.

Maps of the future

Written into the Spiritualists' seven principles – the basic tenants of their religion, which were dictated through trance mediumship – is the important statement "Personal Responsibility". This implies free will. And with any prediction about the future it's important to stress this. The future is not unchangeable. What you see is the potential of the moment – but we can change it.

This is harder on a global scale as it takes the collective wills of thousands, but on the individual's path it is quite easy. The psychic is there to advise the best path to take to good fortune.

It's like a spiritual map that you, the psychic, see from a transcendental viewpoint. Some roads lead to gloomy valleys, some to happy plains. And some places, like cities, have many roads leading to them. Destiny may try to draw the person here. You, as the psychic, are the signpost at the crossroads. Make all your predictions with compassion, always advising which path leads to the greatest spiritual growth. Advise your sitter that the future is what they make it. They can be in control of their potential destiny. Or, in the words of H G Wells's Mr Polly, "If you don't like your life you can change it." You are there to help read the blueprints.

Larry Grayson

In 1971 when Devon-based clairvoyant Helen Edden predicted that the relatively unknown comedian would become a household name, he didn't believe it. "That's ridiculous," Larry stated at the time. But Helen was right. The following year he was invited to appear at the London Palladium. Later the comedian invited Helen to appear on his own TV show as a guest.

Larry is quite psychic himself. Soon after his mother passed he saw her standing by his bed. "I have missed you," he told her. She replied, "I'm quite alright. I'm very happy." "I've seen my mother and she looks marvellous," said Larry. "I've never worried about her from that day to this."

(P N 7 / 8 / 9 3)

Why oracles work

All oracles, techniques for predicting the future, are based upon interpreting random events. The fall of coins or runes, the patterns in sand or smoke stains on a mirror – all are connected with a random element. The random events take on a special meaning when we ask them to be our oracle. Carl Jung, the father of analytical psychology, called this sychronicity. His theory, in simple terms, proposed that psychological events ran in parallel to material ones. Hence, the powerful unconscious psyche attracted unusual coincidences. Oracles are a focal point for these forces.

Understanding the tarot

At first glance the tarot seems hard to understand. Unfortunately, few books explain it simply. They overload the novice with too much information: astrology, psychology, symbolism, numerology, Quabala etc. But the cards were first designed when most of the population was illiterate. Much of the knowledge was passed down by Romany oral traditions.

In essence the cards are only triggers to your own intuition. Some of the best readers I've met don't understand the history and complex mystical traditions and symbolism of tarot. Instead they intuitively grasp the hidden meaning of the cards, and this is what the ancient inventors intended.

This is how I'll teach you to work. You can read up on the rest at your leisure.

Let the tarot teach you

First, you've got to decide which cards you want to work with. I would strongly suggest the Rider pack designed by A E Waite. Their advantage is that they retain much of the traditional symbolism, and all of the cards have a picture to guide you. The cards teach you by themselves.

Before you start practising, get to know the cards. Look at each one and decide what it is trying to tell you. How would you interpret the card in a reading? What does it say about the emotional, spiritual or material conditions of a person? Devote a good deal of time to this before you look up the standard meanings of the cards. It will help you link your own intuitive response to the cards. When you've decided on your interpretation, compare it with the list printed later. You'll probably find that your interpretation comes pretty close to the established meanings.

The basics of tarot

There are 78 cards divided into two main groups: 22 Major Arcana numbered 0 to 21 and 56 Minor Arcana divided into four suits. (Arcana means secret.) The Major Arcana take dominance over the Minor Arcana in a reading. Some novices prefer to begin using only the Major Arcana cards, get to know these, and then introduce the rest of the pack later.

The cards can be shuffled so that they are upright or reversed and the cards' meaning then changes. My feeling is that the cards contain an equal balance of positive and negative imagery anyway and that reversing cards adds little to the overall reading. I rarely use reversed cards and for a beginner it overcomplicates the issue.

The Major Arcana

Here are the traditional meanings:

0. The fool:	Youthful folly, innocence, blinded by ignorance, listen to warnings, the novice.
1.The magician:	Self-control, skill, action, taking charge.
2. The high priestess:	Intuition, wisdom, mysteries, secrets, tenacity.
3. The empress:	Fertility, abundance, mother, health, kindliness.
4. The emperor:	Willpower, ambition, stability, father, benefactor.
5. The hierophant:	Marriage, good advice, religion, the higher self, mercy.
6. The lovers:	Love, sexual union, beauty, emotional success, trials overcome.
7. The chariot:	The driving force, triumph, war, vengeance, providence.
8. Strength:	Fortitude, courage, energy, success, self-discipline.
9. The hermit:	Prudence, a lonely spiritual quest, treason, caution, inertia.
10. Wheel of fortune:	The hand of fate, a turn for the better, luck, destiny, abundance.
11. Justice:	The law, truth, balance, control, a contract.
12. The hanged man:	Wisdom in difficulties, self-sacrifice, intuition, initiation, prophecy.
13. Death:	Transformation, events beyond your control, ending corruption, a new but difficult start, inevitable major changes (the tarot will not predict an actual death).

14. Temperance:	Management, economy, spirit transcending matter, moderation, wise counsel.
15 The devil:	Anger, violence, jealousy, greed, deceit, instinct, sexual passion.
16. The tower:	Catastrophe, repossession, ruin, adversity, calamity.
17. The star:	Hope, goals, expectations, guiding force, enlightenment, bright prospects.
18. The moon:	Dark forces, nightmares, illusion, hidden fears, danger overcome through intuition.
19. The sun:	Happiness, joy, rebirth, freedom, happy marriage, success.
20. The last judgement:	A major decision, outcome, final result, rebirth, problems overcome.
21. The world:	Successful completion, assured success, recognition, long distance travel, harmony.

The Minor Arcana

The Minor Arcana is divided into four suits:

Wands: Covers intellectual activities and career.

Cups: Represents emotions, love, pleasure and sensitivity.

Swords: Involves struggles, difficulties and illness.

Coins: Deals with material world, finances and property.

There are four court cards to each suit: King, Queen, Knight, and Page. These can represent real people or aspects of the personality of the person consulting the cards. (The person consulting the oracle is normally known as the querant.) Pages and Knights can represent children or young people of either sex. The Aces indicate the beginning of a new activity and the cards from two to ten represent aspects of the querant's life — past, present and future.

Overleaf are the basic meanings for the minor cards:

Wands

Ace: A new job or enterprise, initiative, ideas, invention.

2: Dissatisfaction with material things, restlessness, thinking about events happening elsewhere.

3: Overseas trade, planned travel, commerce, established strength.

4: Celebration, country life, socializing, prosperity, peace and concord.

5: Petty arguments between groups of people, a sham fight, squabbles.

6: Victory achieved, good news, the support of others, recognition.

7: Valour, winning against the odds, overcoming opposition, getting on top of your troubles.

8: Communication, a message or letter, swiftness, a speedy conclusion.

9: An uncomfortable wait, gathering strength, problems still to be dealt with.

10: Oppression, a burden that's hard to carry, overwork, emotional pressure, unpleasant news.

King: A clever, honest man who gives good advice.

Queen: An astute woman with a good business sense.

Knight: Change of residence, an enterprising young person.

Page: Good news announced, faithful young person or child.

Cups

Ace: The beginnings of emotional happiness, a new love or re-kindling of marriage, joy, contentment, fertility.

2: Emotional and spiritual love, love blessed by heaven.

3: Celebration, merriment, good friends.

4: Discontentment or depression may cause the loss of a golden opportunity, weariness.

5: Crying over spilt milk, opportunity is at hand and there are new bridges to cross.

6: Childhood memories or friends bring happiness, happy childhood.

7: Fantasy and illusion distract the seeker.

8: Putting the past behind you, a brave but difficult decision.

9: Satisfaction guaranteed – but beware of complacency.

10: Ecstatic personal and family happiness.

King: Sensitive and creative fatherly man.

Queen: Sensitive, visionary woman. Can sometimes get depressed.

Knight: The grail knight. Romantic, artistic, imaginative. A message of love.

Page: A sensitive youngster, a bright idea, news.

Swords

Ace:	Triumph of the will, the start of a forceful attitude.
2:	A decision that requires an unprejudiced attitude, intuitive understanding, amnesty.
3:	Heartache, rupture, division, delay.
4:	Rest, retreat and solitude, a time of recovery.
5:	Dishonour and loss, betrayal by friend.
6:	Travel or holiday, scaping difficulties.
7:	Theft, deceit, trickery, beware of impostor.
8:	Frustration, imprisonment, criticism and sickness.
9:	Worry, despair and neurosis, bad dreams and pressing problems.
10:	Failure, tears, sadness or illness. But the worst is over and a new dawn comes.
King:	Critical man in authority, whose decision is final.
Queen:	Sorrowful woman in authority, who understands pain and sadness.
Knight:	A ruthless person, who acts quickly and will try to twist the law to their advantage.
Page:	An untrustworthy younger person, a spy who will stab you in the back.

Coins

Ace:	A golden opportunity, abundance and improved financial prospects.
2:	Emotional ups and downs, juggling the finances.
3:	Skills appreciated, esteem, honour and reward.
4:	Saving money, caution with money, covetousness, wealth invested wisely.
5:	Poverty and hardship, material troubles, entangled relationship, spiritual poverty.
6:	Gifts, presents, help at hand and generosity. Don't let money pass through your fingers.
7:	Impatience, things will come in the fullness of time, anxiety about money.
8:	Success achieved by hard work, skills in craft and business, job improvements.
9:	A legacy, unearned money, material contentment, rewards, pleasure.
10:	Stable home, riches, family life, success achieved.
King:	Wealthy intelligent man, valour, stability.
Queen:	Serious, intelligent, motherly woman. Opulence, security, generosity.
Knight:	Dependable, responsible man, a bank manager or investor, hard work, perseverance.
Page:	An ambitious young person, success in study and career, management skills, materialist.

Tarot Layout – The Celtic Cross

3
Intentions

10
Future
Outcome

9
Hopes and
Fears

1 Influences

6
Near Future

2
Opposition

5
Past

8
Environment

4
Inner
Feelings

7
Attitude

Your interpretation counts

The above list is only a guide. Some packs may emphasize symbols that are different to the Waite pack. Other writers may have different opinions to mine. In the end, it's up to you to establish your own meanings for the cards. They are a flexible symbolic focus for your intuition.

Lastly, it is almost impossible to read the tarot for yourself: wishful thinking and inner fears get in the way. Again, like all psychic gifts, it is given to you to share with others.

Reading the tarot

The illustration left, shows the most commonly used divinatory spread, called The Celtic Cross. Each position of the cards represents an aspect of the life of the enquirer, or querant (person seeking guidance). If there's a particular question to be asked, select a card that most represents the problem and lay it in the significator position under card I. A person is represented by one of the court cards. If it's a general reading I tend to omit the significator card.

Ask your sitter to shuffle the cards and concentrate on the problem they want guidance for. Lay the cards out face upwards as shown in the illustration. The positions are interpreted as follows:

Card 1. "This covers him"
This card represents the influences on the enquirer or the theme of the problem.

Card 2. "This crosses him"
These are the obstacle in the way. A positive card will show that there is little opposition – but even the favourable cards have some minor negative symbolism.

Card 3. "This crowns him"
This represents the conscious plans and intentions.

Card 4. "This is beneath him"
The card here indicates the person's inner feelings, subconscious desires and state of mind.

Card 5. "This is behind him"
Influences that are passing away are shown by this card. Interestingly sometimes this card represents the nature of the person's life history.

Card 6. "This is before him"
This represents the immediate future events.

Card 7. "This is himself"
This signifies the enquirer's attitude.

Card 8. "This is his environment"
This signifies other people's attitude to the enquirer and home and work influences.

Card 9. "These are his hopes and fears"
This card is influenced by card three to the left. It shows how his hopes and fears influence his intended goals.

Card 10. "This is the outcome"
Or rather the potential outcome if the trends indicated by the cards are adhered to.

The psychic way to read the tarot

Sadly, many tarot readers are clairvoyantly ungifted. The cards will provide interesting insights, but if you want to astonish your sitter with your accuracy, then you must use your clairvoyant skills — which is what this book's all about.

A lot of sitters don't understand that a true psychic doesn't need cards to tell them all about their life and future. When the sitter sees the cards before them, it is reassuring — if the cards say so, then it must be true. I use the cards with some sitters because it focuses their attention, they relax and their aura opens. They are also a useful talking point to keep the attention on the subject being discussed. But the cards are secondary to the psychic gifts you use.

It's interesting to conduct a reading with all the cards face down. I've experimented by placing my hand on the unseen card and told the person all about their life. For example, I place my hand on card number one and describe the sitter's problems. Then for number two I explain the

things that stand in their way, for number three I describe their ambitions, for four their inner feelings, etc. When I turn the cards over it's clearly seen that the images reflect the points I've been talking about.

The fact is that it's the psychic skills that count. Trust your gut feeling. You don't need to look up the meanings of the cards in long lists. You just trust your clairvoyant instincts.

Preparing to read the cards

Before you begin your reading, prepare yourself. Retire to a quiet room and tune yourself in. You may first want to start by doing a few breathing exercises to help quieten your body and mind. Next open your chakras and aura as you did on page 55. Once you've done this, you can do as many readings as you want. But remember afterwards to clear yourself and close the aura down again.

Most people consulting you will be tense. They may have been worrying about what you're going to say since the time they booked their reading. They may have just driven through the rush hour. So help them relax, perhaps with a cup of tea and some idle chit-chat. Reassure them that you won't tell them anything that will frighten them and that they can ask you questions if in doubt, and remind them that the things you will say are the *potential* not the *actual* future.

If they start trying to feed you with information or begin telling you their problems, stop them. Explain that you'll tell them these things during the reading. Knowing too much about the person will distract your intuitive flow. And, after all, you want to be a real psychic – not some charlatan that feeds back information that the sitter has told them. (We call these "cold readings".)

STRANGE PSYCHIC STORIES OF THE STARS

Ronald Searle

The famous cartoonist Ronald Searle awoke one night to see an old American female friend who had passed ten years earlier. "Ronald, Sid's dead," she said referring to her husband. She then disappeared. The next day there was a phone call from New York: Sid had passed during the night.

(PN 18/11/89 & Daily Telegraph)

Reading the tarot

1 Ask your sitter if there's a specific problem they want to ask about or if they'd like a general reading. Choose a significator card to represent it and place it on the table. You can choose a court card to represent the sitter if you like. Ask them to shuffle the cards. Now lay them out face upwards in the way previously indicated.

2 Before considering the cards, tune in to the person. Ask if you can hold something they've owned for some time: their watch, bracelet, etc. Now use the psychometry skills you've already practised to describe their character and life history. Extend your sensing to their aura. You may see the colours and feel their vibration. Tell them about the impressions you feel. Starting in this way links your psychic senses to those of the sitter.

Once you've dried up (if you're any good you could probably continue indefinitely), turn your attention to the cards.

3 First look to see which cards dominate most. Lots of cups may indicate that their problems are emotional, wands link with work, coins with money and swords with strife. These are the pointers to indicate which subjects you should be talking about.

4 Now look at the individual cards. Start with card number one, which covers the person – the theme of the spread. Supposing it's the tower, a very negative-looking card and a symbol of shock and ruin. Telling the sitter the face value meaning won't be very reassuring. You need to dig deeper.

5 Touch the card, close your eyes and watch the images appearing in the third-eye. The tower could have many meanings: emotional shock, an accident, a house repossession, a nervous breakdown. Let your intuition guide you, then speak: "Your world's falling apart because you're worried about a teenager leaving home." If you've trusted your intuition you've probably hit the nail on the head. Other cards nearby may hint at what's wrong. Perhaps the card is crossed by a family card like the six or ten of cups. Or maybe a Page card is shown and represents the young adult in question. The cards will tell you lots but your intuition will tell you even more. If you are really switched on you may be able to say the teenager's name – something the cards alone could never tell you.

6 Supposing you turn to the card that crowns the person in position number three. It's the ace of wands – the start of a new enterprise. But what sort? You look to your intuition and draw a blank. No images. No clues. So try placing another card over it from the pack. You draw the eight of coins, a card that relates to work. "Your son is hoping to start a new job, I see." Ask as you draw the next card if it will be a success. You draw the star. "The new job is very hopeful. You should encourage him. It's a blessing."

7 I place two or three cards over the original card draw to add detail to the reading. The first card drawn is, however, the most significant so don't

overdo it or you'll confuse the reading with too many images to take into account. Again there are no hard-and-fast rules and you can even develop your own methods or layout.

8 Consider all the other cards and the meaning of the position they occupy. Then see how they work with adjoining cards and how they relate to each other and the significator. Let your logical, everyday mind take a back seat. Your intuition will make connections between the images and symbols you see before you. Combine this with the psychic impressions from your sitter and you will give readings that astound people.

Storm in a teacup

Tasseography, the art of reading teacups, has been around for centuries. The Chinese are said to have invented it and the Romans used to read the residue left from the lees of their wine. The gypsies have practised the art, it's a fashionable pastime in America, and even Catholic countries like Ireland have their psychic cup-gazing grandmothers.

The fact that most people see it as entertainment means that it gives you a chance to introduce your psychic abilities to a wider audience. You can turn an after-dinner distraction into a life-changing insight.

By now you should have a better understanding of how to open the aura. Clearly, in the casual social setting in which tea-leaf reading takes place, it would be inappropriate to ask if you can be excused for half an hour to tune yourself in. It's possible, however, to open the aura quickly.

Opening the aura quickly

Instead of sitting in meditation and raising the light through the chakras, visualize a light going directly from the base of your spine to the third- eye in the centre of your forehead. If you've been practising the complete method to open your aura described in Chapter 3 you will have found it becoming easier to "open-up". As you proceed with your reading, the rest of your aura and chakras will open spontaneously. Again, remember to spend some time closing yourself afterwards. If circumstances prevent this, use the visualization image described on page 60 of covering yourself with a dark hooded cloak.

Reading tea-leaves

I once visited the factory of Britain's biggest tea suppliers to discuss designing a set of tea cards about tasseography. I learned from the blenders that "the bigger the leaf the better the tea". In fact, the images formed in tasseography require a large leaf too. Most tea bags contain too much dust if split open, so if you want good tea and a good leaf for reading, select a big-leafed, expensive, loose tea. Alternatively, if you're a fan of Chinese food, try the following techniques with the green or jasmine china teas supplied in restaurants.

Choose a teacup with a wide mouth and gently sloping sides. Fill your sitter's cup without using a strainer. As this is to be used as an oracle, the enquirer must of course drink the tea themselves. Ask them to leave just enough liquid in the bottom so that the residue can be swirled. This is done by taking the cup in the left hand and swirling three times in a clockwise direction. Then invert the cup in the saucer and allow it to drain.

The vertical position in the cup is taken as an indication of time. The handle represents the enquirer, and leaves that fall here affect them closely and are close to fulfilment. Images that cling towards the rim of the cup are in the present, with those in the future towards the bottom. The actual bottom of the cup is considered as the remote future.

Before considering the individual leaf pictures, take a look at the cup as a whole:

❖ A great many leaves means a full and perhaps complicated life.

STRANGE PSYCHIC STORIES OF THE STARS

Lucille Ball

American comedy star Lucille Ball decided to star in the "I Love Lucy" shows after help from "dead" actress Carole Lombard. The possibility of Miss Ball moving from films to TV was regarded as a major risk. When the delicate decision had to be made, Miss Ball heard the actress's voice: "Go on, honey, take the chance." She did – and made TV history.

Lucille could also see the future. She had a premonition that all was not well with Jimmy, the husband of her stand-in and close friend, Helen Thurson. She rang her to express her fears but was reassured that everything was all right. Ten minutes later her phone rang, "Lucy . . .It's Jimmy!" said Helen in a choked voice. "But how in God's world did you know?"

(PN 13/5/89)

- ❖ A few leaves suggests tidiness and self-discipline.

- ❖ Droplets of liquid clinging to the sides represents tears (most upturned cups tend to have this).

- ❖ A clogged mass of leaves spells trouble ahead.

- ❖ Leaves that form letters represent peoples initials.

- ❖ A long, thin trail of leaves indicates a journey.

- ❖ Shapes of people suggest partnerships.

- ❖ Bird shapes indicate good news.

Interpreting the symbols

The pictures made by the leaves are symbols. If you look up their meanings in specialist books, you'll see that there are many discrepancies. Everybody has a different opinion. And this is quite natural: just like in dreams, which you'll learn about later, symbols change their meaning depending on their context and personal associations.

It's best to use your intuition to interpret the meanings. So, supposing you see an anchor, ask yourself what it represents. An anchor stops a ship drifting with the tide; we call people who support us our anchor; if our life feels like it is drifting aimlessly we need an anchor to hold us steady, such as a partner, a job, a home. It's clearly a symbol of stability, although of course it could represent to the enquirer travel by sea.

Animals are often pictured in the leaves. A dog, for example, may represent an actual dog as well as those qualities of friendship, domesticity and loyalty. A ferocious dog could symbolize fear or uncontrolled instincts. Interpret each image as a symbol about the person's life.

As with the tarot cards, you have to dig below the surface meaning. They are clues onto which you can link your psychic awareness. If you've opened your aura, your mental associations will link with your sitter's subconscious.

You pick up their hopes, fears, and plans for the future. And the precognitive skills that you have been developing will be triggered to see the blueprint of events influencing their lives.

Again, don't make alarming predictions. Remind your sitter about the power of free will. Make sure that the things you say will help them to avoid misfortune and to be determined to persevere towards good fortune. Every reading should leave the sitter emotionally stronger, with positive goals set for the future.

Cloud reading

Do you remember, as a child, gazing at cumulus clouds floating through a clear blue sky and recognizing shapes of faces and scenes in them? This is a form of what psychologists call "active imagination". The pictures you see reveal the thoughts of your subconscious mind. It's a form of daydreaming.

Not only does cloud gazing reveal much about your inner world but it can be used, like any random event, as a form of fortune telling. Next time you sit in your deckchair absorbing the sun, try asking the clouds a question about your future.

Your subconscious mind will reveal itself in the clouds. Interpret the symbols in the same way as you did the tea-leaves. You will gain an insight into your hopes and fears as well as possible suggestions for future events and actions. But don't get too serious about it all: remember that, like all oracles that you read for yourself, your thoughts can be prejudiced by your inner hopes and fears.

STRANGE PSYCHIC STORIES OF THE STARS

Elvis Presley

Elvis Presley is said to have foreseen his own tragic death when looking at the pictures formed by cumulus clouds passing by. Also, it's claimed by Elvis's former wife, Priscilla, that Elvis has returned from beyond the grave. She heard noises coming from the stable and went out to check. She saw Elvis's favourite horse upset by a "shimmering form hovering" nearby.

Another intriguing experiment you can try is to exercise your psychokinetic abilities. In 1956 Dr Rolf Alexander, a London physician, demonstrated, in a public test, his ability to influence cloud shapes by thought. Sceptical journalists watched him concentrate on a three-cloud group. His plan was to maintain the position of the two smaller clouds while dispelling the third large one. To everyone's amazement the smaller clouds increased in size and the big one became smaller. It really does work. Try it yourself.

Sand reading

Aborigines, Tibetans, Bedouin nomads and North American Indians all used sand as part of their ritual for prophecies. The random patterns left in sand disturbed by animal tracks across them were interpreted by the shamans as portents for the future. A similar technique is used by modern-day psychics for fortune telling.

To do this you need fine sand in a tray on a table. Spread the sand flat by running a ruler across it. The enquirer should sit opposite you and focus his mind on the question he wants to answer.

Next he has to mark the sand. Some psychics prefer the sitter to mark the sand by randomly brushing the sand's surface with a stick. This has the advantage in that occasionally the marks will reveal letters, crosses and linear shapes to interpret. However, if the sitter is self-conscious, they may leave you with only a few light markings, which gives you less images to interpret.

A better technique is simply to ask your sitter to use their hands and fingers to disturb the sand's surface.

The technique of sand reading is very similar to tea-leaf reading. The undulations in the surface will suggest pictures that you interpret as images and symbols that represent aspects of the person's life. Read the sand in the same way as you did tea-leaves.

Images that fall on your left are symbolic of events in the past, while those on the right are events for the future. Symbols that fall near the sitter's side of the table represent events that will touch him personally and those that fall on your side are events that affect people around him.

The crystal ball

Just like the sand and tea-leaves, a crystal ball acts as a focus for concentration. The images from your subconscious are projected into its interior and you interpret what you see as symbolic or as actual events. Only about one person in 20 has the necessary powers of concentration or is psychically sensitive enough to see the images. But persevere – if you've managed with some of the experiments so far, you're probably one of the few that have the gift.

A perfectly clear quartz crystal ball is the best. (As you know, quartz crystal amplifies psychic energies.) However, glass is cheaper and many scryers prefer Nostradamus's simple bowl of water (page 99). Wash your crystal ball to clear its vibrations and keep it away from strong light and wrapped in black velvet when not in use.

It's important to get in the right state of mind before you give a reading. Meditate for a while, do some breathing exercises to still the thoughts and, as usual, open your aura.

The crystal ball is like a psychic TV screen in which you'll see moving pictures, colours and images. Hold the crystal in your hands on a small square of black velvet. Empty your mind and gaze into it. Just like when you looked at the aura, it's a gentle way of looking – gaze gently rather than staring.

The first signs of success come when, after about five minutes, the ball appears to become milky-white. You may see coloured lights appear; interpret these in the same way as you would the colours of the aura. Some images may be symbolic and can be interpreted as you did with tea-leaf reading. The moving, sequential images are the most interesting. Report what you see to the sitter – they may have a bearing on past or future events. The traditional interpretation is that images moving to the right are symbolic and those to the left are an actual event. Faces seen may be of the living or from the spirit.

Some psychologists say that the images seen in the crystal are a form of eidetic imagery. This ability to stare at an object and then mentally project it onto a wall or screen is often observed in young children. In the past, children were considered the best crystal-gazers. The images seen, say psychologists, may be no more than quasi-visual representations of their own unconscious desires and beliefs.

STRANGE PSYCHIC STORIES OF THE STARS

Cilla Black

Top English TV presenter and singer Cilla Black, writing in *The Daily Star* said that when she clutched her husband, Bobby, "in the middle of the night and told him that I had just seen a ghost in our bedroom, he reckoned I had been dreaming. But I knew I hadn't."

She had seen a 14-year-old phantom with "a very sweet vulnerable face". The ghost wore a mod hat and a Victorian nightdress. Cilla's husband and sons laughed when they first heard Cilla's tale but the girl kept returning.

"I've tried talking to her, but she doesn't answer." she said. Cilla wasn't scared. "Oh please stay, please don't go," called out Cilla the next time the girl appeared.

But Cilla was not the only person to see the ghost. "A friend who didn't know about her asked me who was the young girl he'd seen walking up our stairs in broad daylight." His description fitted the ghost exactly.

(PN 9/2/91)

I agree, but it's through the subconscious that we link with our superconscious psychic abilities. As with all clairvoyant abilities, the subconscious thoughts can get in the way. The fully developed clairvoyant learns to distinguish between his own subconscious thoughts and those entering his consciousness through clairvoyance.

Postal readings

It's debatable whether postal readings are of any real worth. Certainly, it's possible to make a reading over a distance. Jane and I used to have a regular radio show in which we'd make spirit links for telephone callers to the station. There was no woolly evidence — we relayed hard facts about the callers and those they knew in the spirit.

The caller's voice acted as our vibration link. But with postal readings, of course, this isn't possible. However, psychometry skills can be used. The vibrations left on a letter can be read using the skills you've learned. And some psychics like you to send a sample of hair to help strengthen this psychometry link-up. Also, the sender's name can be used to make a numerological interpretation. And some postal readers ask for the date of

STRANGE PSYCHIC STORIES OF THE STARS

Mikhail Gorbachev

When Russia's President, Mikhail Gorbachev, consulted a top Soviet psychic, just before his fall from power, it became headline news. It was alleged that Gorbachev smuggled a blind clairvoyant called Vanga into the Kremlin so she could "read" sugar cubes for him.

The troubled Soviet leader was said to have "quizzed her for two hours on his future" before flying her home to Bulgaria in a government aircraft.

Gorbachev was instructed, by the 79-year-old psychic, to put two sugar cubes under his pillow and leave them for two days before she visited him. Vanga claims she can predict a person's future by touching the cubes. She is well known in Bulgaria for her psychic forecasts.

Gorbachev grew up in a Russian village where to this day superstition, omens and premonitions are taken very seriously. A Kremlin spokesman said, "It's no secret that Gorbachev has been under immense strain recently and this prompted his actions."

Considering events that soon followed, I expect that Vanga's predictions were far from sweet.

Often the newspapers sensationalize stories, and to many readers it must have all sounded a bit silly. But from our studies so far of the ability of crystals to absorb vibration and a psychic's ability to read them with psychometry, there could be some truth in it.

birth so that astrology can be included. In addition, you can cast the tarot cards on the sender's behalf and give an interpretation of their future.

The missing ingredient is the sitter's presence. The auric blending between you is missing. So, if you decide as your abilities increase to try a few postal readings, point this out in your letter or tape. Your reading is a general assessment of the sender's character, hopes and fears. An oracle has been cast and you have used your intuitive skills to interpret it, but this is not an in-depth analysis of their destiny.

Another technique, graphology, involves reading character from the handwriting itself. This can provide an enlightening insight into personality but is not a form of divination nor does it require a psychic gift.

A last word

There are thousands of types of fortune telling. Just about every random event can be used to give a reading. (I know of a psychic that used to read the dirty dishes!) Hopefully, you've realized after reading this chapter that there's more to it than looking up the meanings in books. You have to use your psychic sense, which is triggered by your intuition. Master this and you can use virtually any oracle in about ten minutes.

Chapter 8

Numerology

Think lucky and you'll be lucky. Positive thinking, using the subconscious and the magic of numbers are all ways to find good fortune.

Everyone wants to know about what will happen to them — as if the future's all mapped out and there's nothing we can do about it. But there's some good news: we *can* change the future. We have free will. You're not stuck with an inevitable destiny. You can make the things you want happen.

Against the odds

It never rains but it pours. Sometimes it seems that the cards are stacked against us and our luck will never change. If bad luck hits us twice we often expect a third problem, as superstition tells us that bad luck runs in threes. For some it's worse than that. The odds of being struck by lightning are about three million to one, yet unlucky Roy Sullivan, a US park ranger, was hit seven times. Friends knew him as the human lightning conductor. Perhaps the best run of *good* luck happened at Monte Carlo. Red came up on the roulette table 28 times in a row. The odds for this happening are a staggering 270 million to one!

Simple laboratory experiments reveal that some people can influence the fall of dice or the numbers appearing on an electronic random-number generator. Psychics also believe that thought can travel outside of ourselves and influence not only other people but even the events that come into our lives. Positive thinking brings positive things to us. By thinking positively we attract good luck and our renewed strength of mind gives us the power to take advantage of good fortune when it arrives.

If you want to be an artist, surround yourself with artists. If you'd like to be a musician, then mix with musicians. If you want success — then seek out other positive thinkers. People whose lives are filled with worry, fear, negative thinking and pessimism are their own worst enemies, and they can hold you back too. They'll try to drag you down into their gloomy pit and discredit your success. Surround yourself with doubting Thomases and soon you'll be influenced by their negative thought patterns. If you want to make a real start at changing your luck you have to begin to believe in yourself. Let no one stand in your way. Avoid the vibrations of negative thinkers as much as you can. Collective thought can be very powerful: it can promote healing, deep spiritual meditation or psychic phenomena, so try to keep company with optimists — people that want you to get on in life and find happiness.

You can make a start at changing your luck, right now, by following a few of our simple techniques.

Programme yourself for good fortune

Make a resolve right now to ban forever negative phrases such as "I'll be happy when . . ." or "If only . . . " or "I can't . . . " or "It's not like me . . . ". Instead of focusing on your problems, focus on solutions to problems. Worry wastes energy and holds you back. Also, don't see failure as an obstacle. Adversity is your guru, your teacher. See failure as an opportunity to grow and learn.

Another simple technique is to project an attitude of total self-confidence, no matter what happens. You may be screaming with worry inside but act out your life as if there is nothing bothering you and you can deal with anything life throws at you. It'll influence the people around you to be positive, and you'll trick yourself into actually being that positive, unruffled person you would like to be.

Changing the Inner Software

If we want to change our luck we must first change ourselves. The mind is a powerful tool that, like a computer, can be programmed to transform our lives. To do this, we must work on ourselves on three levels: the subconscious, conscious and super-conscious.

The Subconscious

Rattling around in our subconscious minds are forgotten memories of all our past failures: memories that go right back to early childhood when your parents told you "you can't do that" or "be good and behave". This deep-set conditioning goes on influencing us right into adult life.

But we can change all that. The subconscious responds to repetition until new behaviour patterns are established. In the East, for centuries, they have recognized the power of repetitive phrases, or mantras. Now many people in the West, and in particular those associated with the New Age movement in the United States, use repetition to influence behaviour in the form of what are known as "affirmations".

Try, at first, choosing one from our list printed here but later experiment with your own ideas. You can buy books of "spiritually charged" affirmations but there's no reason you can't make up your own affirmation. Make it full of imagery with powerful wording. Repeat it to yourself whenever you can, such as when you are ironing or doing a dull task; particularly repeat it before you go to sleep.

Some positive affirmations:

Willpower: I will never ever give up. No matter what difficulty knocks me down I will stand again and fight. I will never, never, give up.

Health: My spirit is untouched by illness. My spirit body is perfect. I am whole. Perfect health is mine to have.

Wealth: Nature is endlessly abundant. All things shall come to me in the fullness of time.

Happiness: It is my divine right to be happy. No event or person will block my path to perfect happiness. I am happy now and will be for all eternity.

The Conscious

Opportunity often passes us by because we don't plan our lives properly. Salesmen are well aware of the importance of setting goals to reach their sales targets, and we can use the same techniques to achieve our life goals. Use your conscious mind to plan ahead. Set yourself short-term realistic goals, together with long-term objectives and put a time limit on them.

Every day write a 'today list'. Make it realistic and achievable and do the most difficult task on your list first. Also set yourself a goal for the week, for the months, for the year and so on into your future. The tasks will be bigger the further you go forward. For example, you may set yourself the goal of having a bigger house within five years. Plan ahead and know that what you want *will* come to you.

The Super-conscious

Psychics and mystics believe that we are part of a universal mind and that through meditation we can influence the very events that come into our lives. When we meditate we set up powerful forces that go out from ourselves to influence the world around us. So choose your goals carefully and be sure that they are what you really want from life. Our ultimate goal should be to achieve happiness for ourselves and others: happiness is the highest level of success.

Sit quietly and let your breathing and thoughts become still. Find your quiet inner space. Now imagine the psychic centre in the middle of your forehead opening as a shining light. Visualize yourself enjoying the goal that you wish to achieve. For example, if your goal is a happy family, see yourself and your family members all smiling and enjoying each other's company. You may want to set your vision in a happy context such as around the Christmas table or walking on a summer's day through the countryside. Build the image in your mind, sense the colours, smells and sounds and know deep in your heart that this visualization is possible. Use the power of your will to influence the universal mind. This is a very

---

STRANGE PSYCHIC STORIES OF THE STARS

Elizabeth Taylor

Liz was born under an unlucky star – or so the history of her life has proved. Broken marriages, illness and trauma have filled her life. It is said that "diamonds are a girl's best friend" but not so in Liz Taylor's case. The fabulous diamond, bought at great expense by the late Richard Burton, brought nothing but unhappiness in its wake. Perhaps, like many famous jewels throughout history, the diamond was cursed. Much of Liz's bad luck started from the moment she was given it. Certainly, its previous owner, an arms dealer, must have infused it with bad karmic vibrations.

powerful technique that will influence the forces of your life and can transform it for the better.

Numerology

Numbers have always been associated with good or bad luck. They also can tell us a great deal about our destiny. Some numbers have had good or bad associations for centuries. Seven, for example, has always been considered lucky. The Babylonians recognized the existence of seven celestial bodies: the Sun, the Moon, Mercury, Mars, Venus, Jupiter and Saturn. Christian traditions inherited similar associations with seven. The four material elements, earth, air, fire and water, combine with the spiritual number three — the holy trinity. Seven thus links spirit with matter.

Twelve, in the pre-Christian Middle East, was considered a number of harmony because it represented the 12 signs of the Zodiac. Thirteen, however, disrupts the balance and was therefore unlucky. Again, Christianity absorbed this tradition. There were 13 people present at the Last Supper — Jesus and his 12 disciples. The 13th disciple, Judas Iscariot, betrayed his master. Mexicans, however, consider 13 a lucky number. In Italy 17 is considered the number of misfortune.

The superstitious Chinese see eight as the luckiest number of all. Take a look at the car numberplates of Chinese businessmen — there is usually an eight in the plate.

Numerologists, who study the mystical significance of numbers, believe that numbers reveal a great deal about our fortunes and personalities. Some of the most significant numbers are those derived from our name. There are three main numbers that can be extracted:

The Soul Number, which is obtained by adding the numerical total of the vowels, signifies our inner self.

The Persona Number, obtained from the total of consonants, and represents how others see you.

Sir Alec Guinness

Sir Alec Guinness met "rebel" actor James Dean at his Hollywood home on 23 September 1955 and was shown Dean's latest car — a Porsch Spyder. Sir Alec felt uncomfortable, "then I had this premonition," he explained. "I said, 'Please do not drive that car. I have a feeling that if you do you will be dead within a week'." He died exactly a week later.

(PN 26/12/87)

The Name Number, derived from the whole name, signifies your path through life and your fundamental personality traits.

How to work out your Name Number

Let's convert your name into a number. You don't need to include your middle name(s). Choose the name you are known by. For example, if your name is Susanna Samantha Smith but everyone knows you as Sue Smith, then use Sue Smith to work out your name number. (It's interesting to compare a maiden name with a married name to see how a person has changed. But it's the name you were born with that has the greatest significance.)

Here's how to do it. Write your name on a piece of paper and convert each letter to a number from the table below.

1	2	3	4	5	6	7	8	9
A	B	C	D	E	F	G	H	I
J	K	L	M	N	O	P	Q	R
S	T	U	V	W	X	Y	Z	

So Sue Smith becomes:

S	U	E		S	M	I	T	H		
1	+3	+5		+1	+4	+9	+2	+8	=	33

Add the digits in the result together, if the sum is still more than one digit, add the digits together again, so you wind up with just one digit: $3 + 3 = 6$.

Name and Number

Now look up what your Name Number says about you. It will be one of the numbers from 1 to 9 — a summary of the personality traits and approach to life associated with each is given here.

1: The initiator

You are full of bright ideas and love freedom and independence. You're an individualist, dress in the latest fashions and want a good job before a permanent relationship. Sometimes you can be a bit stubborn. Career matters more than relationships and you are a pillar of strength in difficult times. Beware of arrogance or selfishness. If good luck comes your way be sure to share it with others.

Lucky numbers: 1, 10, 19, 28, 37, 46, 55, 64, 73, 82, 91, 100
Lucky day: Sunday
Some number ones: Socrates, Mahatma Gandhi, Plato, Harrison Ford, Marilyn Monroe, Bridgitte Bardot

2: The attractive one

Balance is your goal. You look forward to marriage and children. Two is a symbol of partnerships and combining opposites, so you could also be a good diplomat. You like artistic things and you dress accordingly. You are gentle, passive and artistic. Peace and harmony are important to you. Your powers of intuition are great but you need to guard your over-sensitivity. Use your natural intuition to follow the hidden path that fortune opens for you.

Lucky numbers: 2, 11, 20, 29, 38, 47, 56, 65, 74, 83, 92
Lucky day: Monday
Some number twos: Leonardo da Vinci, Lord Byron, Christopher Columbus, Steve Martin, William Shatner, Tom Hanks, Benny Hill, Mel Brooks

3: The communicator

You know how to communicate and put your imagination into action. You'd make a good actor or actress, and friends are attracted by your enthusiasm and energy. You have a tendency to exaggerate. You think positively and you easily achieve success. You are also naturally lucky. Be careful not to waste your energy. When lady luck favours you, be sure not to waste your opportunity.

Lucky numbers: 3, 12, 21, 30, 39, 48, 57, 66, 75, 84, 93
Lucky day: Thursday
Some number three's: Horatio Nelson, Richard Nixon, Yuri Gagarin, Spencer Tracy, George Foreman, Frank Bruno, Whoopi Goldberg, Robert Mitchum

4: The home builder

Home is where your heart is. You're the home builder: practical, cautious and reliable. You like to build solid foundations for the future but you sometimes overwork. You're good with money but tend to work hard to get it! You are steady and practical with a great endurance. Overwork and stubbornness are your weaknesses. Sometimes good fortune seems slow in coming – but when it does you know how to double it.

Lucky numbers: 4, 13, 22, 31, 40, 49, 58, 67, 76, 85, 94

Lucky day: Sunday

Some number fours: Hippocrates, Archimedes, John Mills, Diane Keaton

5: The voice of experience

You want to explore life and learn as much as you can. New ventures attract you. For you, the grass is always greener on the other side of the mountain. Your quick thinking can sometimes make you highly strung and your curiosity always gets the better of you. You are lively and pleasure-seeking, and an excellent talker with a good sense of humour. Routine jobs bore you and you must learn to be more truthful. Slow down and watch for opportunity. A turn of fate is around every corner but you must learn to grasp good fortune.

Lucky numbers: 5, 14, 23, 32, 41, 50, 59, 68, 77, 86, 95

Lucky day: Wednesday

Some number fives: Michelangelo, Charlotte Brontë, Dionne Warwick, Roman Polanski, Prince Charles, Oprah Winfrey, Bill Clinton, Elvis Presley

STRANGE PSYCHIC STORIES OF THE STARS

James Dean

James Dean's brief life (1931-1955) has become legendary. He died on 30th September 1955, aged 24, in a horrific car accident. On his last trip home, he posed for a photographer by sitting in a coffin in Hunt's Funeral Parlor. Seven months later his mangled body was carried back to the same place in preparation for burial.

The curse of James Dean's car lived on. The wrecked car was bought by George Barris and sent to a garage. As the mechanic unloaded it, the car fell on him and broke his legs.

The engine was bought by Dr Tory McHenry in 1956. His car ran out of control in a race at Pomona Fair Ground and he was killed. The transmission was bought by another doctor – his car overturned and he was seriously injured. Even the tyres, when sold on, blew out simultaneously.

The rest of the car was exhibited by the Californian Highway Patrol as part of a road safety exhibit.

The garage in which Dean's car was stored burnt down, and when the Porsch Spyder was finally displayed, the car fell from its stand and broke a boy's neck.

The car was beginning to get a bad reputation and was transported to Salinas by truck. The truck ran out of control and the driver was flung from the cabin. Dean's car rolled off the back and crushed the cab driver to death.

If anything was a "Rebel without a Cause" it was surely James Dean's unlucky car.

6: Peace and harmony

Sometimes your friends have to drag you out. You love your home and family so much. You can be trusted and make many friends. You are good at the arts, cooking and design. But don't become too much of a recluse. Family harmony is your touchstone but you can sometimes be obstinate. Six is the number of friendship, and in love you are romantic rather than sensual. Your good luck comes through others.

Lucky numbers: 6, 15, 24, 33, 42, 51, 60, 69, 78, 87, 96
Lucky day: Friday
Some number sixes: Robert E Lee, Abraham Lincoln, Julie Andrews, Boris Karloff, T S Eliot, Gloria Estefan, Mel Gibson, Tom Cruise, Richard Gere

7: The philosopher

You like to be alone with your creative thoughts. You could even be a natural psychic. Discos and noisy environments are not for you. You like to listen to people and share their deepest feelings. You have the meditative nature of the mystic. Your intuition and vivid dreams may have already developed into psychic gifts. Your spiritual gift is the key that will attract luck to you.

Lucky numbers: 7, 16, 25, 34, 43, 52, 61, 70, 79, 88, 97
Lucky day: Monday
Some number sevens: George Washington, Isaac Newton, Thomas Edison, Mary Shelley, Demi Moore, George Peppard, Barbra Streisand

8: Lucky you

You love organizing people and would make a good executive. People look to you for leadership. Hard work is the name of the game and you can easily achieve your goals. You will never be poor. You have great will-power. You do not rely on luck and make your own good fortune through hard work. Watch out for your sometimes ruthless nature.

Lucky numbers: 8, 17, 26, 35, 44, 53, 62, 71, 80, 89, 98
Lucky day: Saturday
Some number eights: William Wordsworth, Robert Louis Stevenson, Jack Nicholson, Rod Stewart, Christopher Lee

9: The free spirit

You just love freedom – for everyone. You are the great reformer and will give your time for free if it's a just cause. You're a born winner but can sometimes be a bit quarrelsome. You fight for the rights of others. You are tolerant amd determined, and usually win your battles. Number 9 people are in control of their destiny and use good luck wisely.

Lucky numbers: 9, 18, 27, 36, 45, 54, 63, 72, 81, 90, 99
Lucky day: Tuesday
Some number nine's: Marco Polo, Kublai Khan, Albert Einstein, Anthony Hopkins, Alfred Hitchcock, Woody Allen

What's in a name?

An intriguing experiment with numbers is to consider the changes that happen in a person's life when they *change* their name. Women, of course, change their name when they marry, and showbiz people, artists and writers often use a nom-de-plume. Take, for example, the folk musician we all know as Bob Dylan. Born Robert Zimmerman, his original name reduces, despite its length, to number one. Dylan's early life was typical of a number one personality: formulating new ideas. He hitchhiked through America in Jack Kerouac style, and above all loved his freedom and independence.

His new name, Bob Dylan, had the numerological value of three: the communicator. The influence of the rebellious number one personality was still there but now he could express his beliefs. Bob Dylan's name is synonymous with the outburst of new radicalism that swept America. His songs brought expression to a whole generation's ideas. Dylan became the great communicator.

The year ahead – what the numbers say

Your birthday determines your Year-cycle Number. This repeats every nine years and changes every birthday. To find out which number is influencing you now and your fortunes after this year's birthday, first write down the date of last year's birthday. Supposing it was 19th October 1993. Convert this to numbers and add them together as you did with your name:

$19/10/93 = 1 +9 +1 +0 +1 +9 +9 +3 = 33$

Now add again $3 + 3 = 6$

The example shows a person currently experiencing a number six year cycle. On their birthday this year, 19/10/94, they enter number seven. 1995 will be a number eight year and so on until we get back to number one again.

Now look up your forecast for your own Year-cycle Number.

1: This is a good time to put the past behind you and make a new start. Simplify things and start putting yourself first. Decisions you make now will have far-ranging effects into the future. It's time to let the world know the real you, and your new attitude may even attract a special person into your life.

2: Keep calm and be receptive. Some people may have their differences and you're the one to sort them out. But decisions now may not be easy and there may be delays. This is the perfect time for tying the knot. Partnerships are very lucky. In work you may receive sudden recognition. This year, long periods of quiet are interrupted by exciting, unexpected activities.

3: A hectic year with lots of opportunity to travel. It's a year of spend, spend, spend, but watch that bank balance carefully. This should be a lucky time. Lots of parties to go to and you'll be surrounded by new friends.

4: There's a lot of work to do this year but it will be well worth it. You'll be preparing a secure future. You will draw close to your partner and may make good investments. If you decide to go on a diet this is the year to work off that excess weight.

5: You're ready for a change and may feel restless. Work will be hectic and you will learn to communicate with others. It's a year of quick thinking and positive action. You will have a magnetic attraction to the opposite sex and life could be quite exciting.

6: A year to get back into balance. You will feel settled and will be looking for long-term romance. Home and family will be important and you will be supportive towards others. You may enjoy the arts or projects that involve groups of people. This is a time when you extend love to friends, family and your partner.

7: A dreamy year ahead. Now's the time when you understand the spiritual side of life. You will feel relaxed and at ease with yourself. Material problems will take care of themselves and you will have time to think. It's also a good time for study.

8: Money just falls into your lap. You should receive promotion at work or a pay rise. You will be confident in everything you do. In relationships you gain a new maturity of attitude. You gain respect and friendship. This is a time of rewards for the hard work you've done in the past.

9: As one door closes, another opens. This is the time to get rid of the old and make way for the new. This year should have many major changes. You will meet many new friends, and old flames may rekindle. Events this year prepare the ground for new opportunities after your next birthday.

Your birth number

One of the most important numbers is your Birth Number as, unlike a name, it never changes. Add the numbers of your date of birth together and reduce them, as before, until they form a one-digit number. This unchangeable number is the governing influence in your life. Look it up in the list of number definitions above and interpret this as the underlying theme of your life and destiny. For example, if you're a number one then your destiny may lie in innovating new ideas. A number two's life will be a search for calm. Threes will travel. Fours will work hard. Fives will be restless throughout life. Sixes will seek balance. Sevens will seek spiritual things whereas eights like money. And if you're a number nine then you're supposed to be working on the highest spiritual level and aiming towards perfection.

If your Birth Number and Name Number are the same, you will be fortunate in life. Some keen numerologists have changed their names by deed pole to ensure success. Also, if your Name Number and Birth Number appear in your birth date, this too is fortunate. Supposing your name number is seven and you were born on the seventh day of the seventh month – you'll be lucky.

Using numbers in your readings

An understanding of numerology can add to your knowledge of oracles. The 22 Major Arcana of the tarot cards each have a number and these are considered as significant in the reading. (Twenty-two is another lucky number, associated with the number of letters in the Hebrew alphabet.) You may feel inclined during a reading to draw your sitter's attention to the numerological meaning of the card that covers them in the spread or of the divinatory meaning of the numbers on the cards that lie in future positions.

Numerology is interesting in its own right. In the last chapter, I presented some ideas for postal readings. If your correspondent has supplied their name and birth date, you have two starting points for a wide range of numerological exercises.

Chapter 9

Dreams

If you're really serious about developing your psychic skills you must get to know your innermost self.

Dreams are an important key to this self-knowledge. They can also be used to programme yourself towards a more positive attitude and bring about greater self-awareness and self-healing. And, most importantly for our purposes, they are a gateway to psychic powers.

In this chapter we'll look at some of the scientific discoveries about dreams, teach ourselves how to understand and influence them and look at how they can be used to predict the future or take us on a journey to the astral plains.

Do you dream?

Believe it or not, we all dream every single night. And they're not nonsense. Dreams reveal our most secret desires. They can be used to solve our most difficult problems and may even tell us about the future. But we need to learn how to remember them if we want to use them to change our lives.

Dream researchers, in the 1950s, noticed that sometimes the eyes of their sleeping subjects would move rapidly from side to side. During these periods of "rapid eye movement" (REM) sleep, dreams were found to be taking place. This discovery enabled scientists to tell how often we dreamed. By waking the subject during REM sleep they could guarantee there would be a dream to study.

The average sleeper dreams every 90 minutes — and the longest dreams, lasting 30 to 45 minutes, occur in the morning. Dreams of a prophetic nature usually occur during the deepest part of our night's sleep; for most of us this will be between 2:00 am and 7:00 am. Try setting your alarm slightly earlier than usual. With luck you'll interrupt a dream, perhaps even one that has something to say about your future. This is a quick and easy way to start getting into the habit of remembering your dreams.

Dreams as problem solvers

Thoughts, ideas, worries, hopes and fears are all represented by symbols, metaphors and images within your dreams. This is the language of your dreams. The subconscious will draw from your experiences and write them into a mini play. A problem of today may be compared to an event from your childhood, or the dream may be influenced by a film you watched before going to bed. And some anxieties, which you'd pushed aside, may return again and again, asking to be resolved.

Most of us are emotionally at the mercy of our troubles. We run from our shadow. But if we use dreams properly we can, with a little effort, become the master of ourselves. You have the key inside your head: the subconscious, your own biological computer.

Dream incubation

Let's programme the inner computer. First examine your problems. There may be many: relationships, work, money, exams, or you may just be stumped for a creative idea. (Many great inventions have been inspired by dreams.) Now select the problem that you most want to resolve tonight. Write it down in the form of a question. Then, just before you go to sleep, put it under your pillow. You've just pressed the first button of your inner computer.

Before falling asleep, run through the question once more in your mind. Try to turn it into picture form. For example, if it's a relationship problem, imagine talking about the question with the person concerned. Keep it fairly positive — you don't want to set up gloomy imagery.

Once you've set the programme running, the dreams will do the rest. Now put the problem out of your mind. Relax and look forward to your dream. Treat it like a letter that you look forward to receiving in the morning.

If you've told yourself to have a dream, you will probably have one. Later, I'll give you some tips about how to remember your dreams and some simple ways of interpreting them. Remember, though — it's how *you* interpret the symbolism that counts. Don't rely on lists in dream books; decide for yourself. Dreams are very personal things. If you decide to talk about one with a friend, pay attention to the way you describe it, references you make, turns of phrase, memories it may trigger. They are all clues to your dream's answer to your question.

Your next step is to make the dream part of your life. Supposing you dreamed of being bullied or insulted. Clearly you need to be more assertive. So choose a keynote for the day. Write it down: "Be assertive." Carry the note with you and experiment in everyday situations. Start practising the dream's advice all day. You will open new doors to self-confidence.

How to encourage dreaming

❖ **Convince yourself:**   Once you have the motive to dream, the rest is easy. Regard your dreams as valuable messages from your inner self.

❖ **Enjoy them:**   You may not win an Oscar but you are the star of your inner play.

❖ **Visualize:**   As you fall asleep imagine yourself waking in the morning feeling pleased that you have had a dream.

❖ **Affirm:**   Tell yourself that you *will* have a dream and *will* remember it.

❖ **Plan:**   Set your alarm at a different time or drink a large glass of water so that you have to wake up in the night.

❖ **Dream yoga:** The Tibetan yogis suggest you should be visualizing a blue light at the back of the throat as you fall asleep. Modern research confirms this. The stem of the brain (behind the throat) controls the dream states.

How to remember your dreams

Most people do not routinely remember their dreams when they wake up in the morning. Some insist that they never dream at all. But scientific studies have proved them wrong. Everybody dreams between four and five times every night.

Why dream memories fade so quickly on waking is not fully understood. Some scientists speculate that we begin forgetting as the dream is taking place. Dream memories only relate to the most recent dream action. But there are some simple ways to help you remember.

The most effective technique is to keep a pen and paper by your bed and write down your first thoughts of the morning. Some people like to expand this further and keep a dream diary. The conscious decision to recall a dream in itself acts as a catalyst to help you remember. Even talking about dreams can be an effective trigger and fragments may occur to you during the day.

You will need to take the time to contemplate your dream. Writing a dream down focuses the attention on its meaning. Ask yourself what each image means to you and what part of your personality it represents. Remember that dreams are symbols. By unravelling the allegories and metaphors, we learn important information to guide us through life's ups and downs.

Above all, make it fun. Don't take yourself too seriously, yet be honest with yourself. In this way you will get to know yourself better and acknowledge those parts of you that until now you may have ignored.

The dream recall checklist

Keep a dream diary

Most dreams are forgotten within 10 minutes, so start writing as soon as you wake up. First give the dream a title. Don't worry about spelling or grammar, it's more important to get your thoughts down on paper. The act of writing will help you remember. Even if you didn't dream, write the first thoughts you have – it may well trigger recall.

List everything, no matter how unimportant it may seem. Record things you heard first as they are the hardest to remember; visual memories are easiest. Then note the day and date. It may be useful later, particularly if your dream was a premonition.

Some people divide the page in two with a vertical line down the centre of the page. On the left they write the dream and on the right the interpretation.

Tell someone

It's surprising how many extra details surface if you talk about your dream. They may also be able to help with the interpretation.

Flash-backs

Fragments of the dream may recur during the day. Make a note of them.

Nightmares

Emotionally charged dreams have a lot to say about your problems. By recalling them you start to face your anxieties and reduce their hold over you. Remember that dreams are symbols – don't take them too literally. Dreams of dying, for instance, signify change and new beginnings. Falling may mean you lack confidence, and being chased shows that there's a problem you've been running away from.

Dreaming of past lives and the future

If you've asked your dream to solve a problem, you may also get a flash of clairvoyance. The dreaming brain looks into the Akashic Record – which, psychics believe, is the blueprint of all that has happened and contains the potential for the future. Some ordinary people have identified past lives with their dreams and have even been able to check the information through the public records. Others have had remarkable prophecies for the future.

The future is flexible. You can change it. If a dream gives you an insight, remember, it's only a potential, so don't get too anxious. There were many cancellations by passengers due to board the *Titanic* who had had ominous dreams about the ship sinking. These dreamers had a premonition. They were warned and so they changed their destinies.

Dreams of the future also use symbolism. Sometimes the picture becomes distorted. You may dream of digging up a lost treasure and receive a promotion the next day. If you're interested in prophecy, highlight them in your dream diary.

Your dream diary will become your book of wisdom and verify your premonitions. It will contain suggestions to solve your problems today, hints to overcome difficulties, and ways to recognize opportunities for the future. Take a tip from Oscar Wilde: "I never travel without my diary. One should always have something sensational to read on the train."

Clairvoyant glimpses

Some dreams are so vivid that they are closer to visions than dreams. These often reveal remarkable predictions about the future. We are not captive to the present. In dreams we become masters of time and can have clairvoyant glimpses of what may come.

The philosophy of "serialism" was first proposed in 1927 by J W Dunne in his book An Experiment with Time. In his view, all events that have ever occurred, that exist now, or ever will exist, are everlastingly in existence. In our waking life we are only aware of the present. In sleep, however, we can have glimpses of the future.

The subconscious translates our insights into a symbolic form. Often an event is distorted or turned into an allegory. But not every dream is a precognition. We must always be careful to distinguish between what is fact and what is our normal dreaming state.

Dunne points out that the sense of "having been here before", which most of us experience at some time in life, is due to a half-remembered precognitive dream. In a recent American poll of psychic experiences over 80 per cent of respondents claimed to have had this experience we call *déjà vu*.

Dreams are a window to view the future. With them we can recognize and avoid dangers, plan and see potential events, and so become masters of our destiny.

Precognition

There's a state between sleeping and waking that psychologists call hypnagogic dreaming. It happens just before you fall off to sleep, and if you've already experienced this you'll know how remarkable it is. These dreams are a flow of brilliant vivid images which, if you can maintain the state, can be manipulated. Hypnagogic dreams contain potent omens of the future.

Many of your "ordinary" dreams may already contain prophecies. If you keep a dream diary as suggested earlier, you can refer to it to see if any of your dreams really have come true.

To stimulate the gift of prophecy it's a good idea to set a target subject to dream about. It is better to choose something that you are not emotionally involved with. So for our experiment we're going to try to predict next week's newspaper headlines.

1 First you must choose a target. Supposing you decide to make a prediction about a famous person or topical event that's currently in the news. Cut out a photo of them or a related photo from your newspaper.

2 Put the photo by the side of your bed before retiring. Touch it so that you focus your attention as you prepare to go to sleep.

3 As you drop off you may notice images flashing before your mind's eye. Try to concentrate on these and retain them.

4 Now visualize the front page of a newspaper. There are no headings yet – it's a blank page. Think again of your target person or scene and make the picture appear on the front page.

5 Does a heading appear also? If so, pull yourself back from the brink of sleep and jot it down. If not, let yourself go and write your dream down in the morning. You may find an accurate prediction is contained in next morning's dream.

The secret life of dreams

There are many theories about the role of dreams but most agree that they are the link between your conscious mind and your unconscious. There's no doubt that they are essential to health and well being. Dreams are a safety valve. They are as important as eating or drinking, for without them our frustrations and anxieties would overwhelm us.

We also learn through dreams. The events of the day are organized and re-assessed. Dreams can show us solutions to our problems and prepare us for the future. And they expose our deepest fears and signpost ways to inner peace.

Symbols are the universal language of dreams. Many psychologists believe in a collective unconscious – a storehouse of ancient symbols that the sleeping mind draws upon. Because of this some dreams are common to all of us. On the next page we've identified and interpreted some of the most frequent themes.

The ancient Egyptians and Greeks believed that dreams were messages from the gods. Like many psychics today, they believed that dreams may hold the keys to the future and reveal the forces of destiny and events that are about to happen. Our next step is to understand our dreams' symbolic language.

Understanding dream symbolism

There are many dreams that we all have in common. Teeth falling out indicates insecurity; fire: transformation; being trapped: frustration; journeys: the path of your life; water: the emotions. But most dreams don't fit into neat categories. They are your unique experience. Here's some questions to ask yourself to find out what *your* dream symbol means to *you*.

"Is the person I dreamed about really me?" Most of the people we dream about represent aspects of ourselves. Supposing your mother is bossy and you dream about her, your dream may be saying you're getting too bossy, just like your mother.

"Does the dream environment represent me?" If you dream of a stormy sea, it may indicate that your emotions are tempestuous. Or a house can symbolize your own body. Is it run down or well kept? A peaceful pastoral scene may indicate inner peace or peace of mind ahead.

"Can I reverse the dream?" Try turning the dream upside down. For example, supposing you dreamed of walking over a carpet with muddy boots, ask yourself, "Am I the carpet being walked on by other people?"

"Are there any puns in the dream?" If you dream of a washing machine it could be a symbol of gossip — washing dirty linen. Or perhaps someone's name is implied. For instance, you dream of using a pencil and it turns out the dream is talking about a friend named Mark.

"Have I dreamed this before?" If so, look back through your dream diary and see what previous problem it related to.

"Does the dream remind me of an event from my life?" What the dream is saying is "you feel happy *just like* the day you got married or you need a break *just like* your holiday in Spain or the pressure you feel is *just like* the day you took your exams at school."

There are many dream themes that we all have in common. Find out what your dream reveals about your hidden self:

Falling

Dreams about falling usually occur as you're "falling off" to sleep. They may be triggered by a drop in blood pressure, a movement of the fluid in the middle ear, or a limb dangling off the side of the bed.

Some psychologists believe that these are archaic memories from the time when we were tree-dwelling monkeys. The ape-men that survived their fall passed on their genes with the memory of the event. The dead ones didn't. And that's why so often you dream of falling but of never hitting the ground.

As a symbol, falling highlights a loss of emotional equilibrium or self-control. You may fear "letting go" in real life. Anxiety usually accompanies this dream. It may represent your insecurity, a lack of self-confidence, a fear of failure or an inability to cope with a situation.

There could also be a literal interpretation. You may have noticed something unsafe – a loose stair rail, wobbly ladder or insecure window. Check it out. The dream may be a warning.

Flying

Sigmund Freud, the father of modern psychology, saw "flying" dreams as a symbol of sexual release. Superstition says that they are lucky and the Babylonians believed they promised great riches ahead.

These dreams are generally very pleasant. When your dreaming spirit soars it means that you've been liberated from an obstruction in your life. You have high hopes and are overcoming obstacles at last.

You must also beware of over-ambition. Don't elevate yourself above others or, you may find a fall follows your rapid rise to success.

STRANGE PSYCHIC STORIES OF THE STARS

Graham Greene

Much of Graham Greene's inspiration for his novels came from dreams. Professor Norman Sherry, his biographer, said that dreams "provided the author with vital stimulus, especially if he found his creative energy flagging".

He went on, "He would wake up and enter it in his diary. I do not think he was a restful sleeper. What was extraordinary was that his dreams were carefully indexed in his spidery handwriting."

Greene's widow, Viviene, said that some of the stories "came to him in dreams. He was interested in them from his early youth when he was being analysed."

Some of Greene's dreams contained prophecies. He foresaw the sinking of the Titanic and is on record as foretelling the death of General Omar Torrijos, the Panamanian president, who died in a plane crash in 1979.

(PN 30/8/91)

Climbing

Ask yourself why you are climbing. Are you escaping from something dangerous in the dream, like a wild animal? Then perhaps your dream symbolizes an escape from bad emotions. Or maybe you're climbing a ladder of success! Fulfilment of ambitions is often symbolized by this dream. If you are filled with a fear of the dizzy heights you may need more self-confidence.

Walls and mountains to climb symbolize obstacles in life that you need to overcome. An easy climb will show success but climbing a precarious mountain ledge means that there's an uphill struggle ahead. Deal with them one step at a time.

Nudity

If you dream of being nude in public you are having a well-known anxiety dream. You may be inhibited and fear sexual relationships. Alternatively, if you're admired in the dream then you may be looking to fulfil your sexual desires.

It can also signify the "naked truth". There may be a feeling of being exposed. Perhaps you fear failure or that you will make mistakes and be ridiculed? In your waking life you need to overcome your feelings of vulnerability and learn self-confidence.

If you dream of being partly dressed, such as going to work without trousers on, you fear that you are not prepared for what lies ahead. Thoroughly examine your plans and perfect them.

Being chased

This is a metaphor for insecurity. Circumstances may be closing in on you or you may be at the mercy of feelings that get out of control. You may have feelings of guilt or a fear of being caught. Ask yourself if you're trying to get away from something in your life. By running away you're refusing to face the truth. The unconscious mind is asking you to tackle a problem that is trying to take control of you.

Children who have this dream may be being bullied at school. Sometimes these dreams highlight our own infantile insecurities. The American Indian witchdoctors used to advise their dreamers to "wake up in the dream" and turn and attack their dream pursuer.

Death

Dreams of death are symbolic. They represent the ending of one phase so that a new one can begin. If it features someone you know, question what aspect of yourself that person represents. For example, has the romantic, angry or impatient person in you died? A dead animal may represent the instinctive part of you – perhaps a repressed part that you must bring back to life.

If you see yourself as a corpse, then it means that you can't cope with your problems and if you dream your partner is dead it warns that all is not right in your relationship. You may want to make some changes.

Treasure

Digging up buried treasure or finding money symbolizes rediscovering a part of yourself. Is there something that you have neglected or repressed? It could be that you had an ambition in life and only now have found the opportunity to try again. There may be a wealth of past experiences that you can draw on.

The dream may also have a literal interpretation. If you're worried about finances, now may be the time to start a new venture. The dream may symbolize other things too: power, independence, or security. Examine your life – there may be unlooked-for opportunities just below the surface.

Sex

Freud believed that all dreams were sexual in nature. Our secret wishes and fears, he believed, are expressed through the symbolism of dreams.

Some dreams are sexually explicit and others cloak eroticism in symbols. Swords, daggers, guns, trains entering tunnels are all phallic symbols. To dream of playing the piano, Freud said, was representative of the rhythm of the sexual act.

Erotic dreams express our sexual fantasies, but don't take them too literally. A dream lover may not necessarily be someone you would wish to sleep with in real life. They may symbolize an aspect of your sexuality that needs to be expressed.

Persistent sexual dreams or dreams of sex with strangers may indicate that you are unfulfilled. You will need to talk frankly with your partner.

Snakes

Snakes are a universal symbol found in the dreams, myths, religion and art of all cultures. They are phallic symbols and have long been linked with pagan fertility gods. The serpent, because it lives in the ground, is also associated with the earth and the underworld. Christian imagery emphasizes the dark side. The snake is the evil tempter of Eve in the Garden of Eden. In dreams it often symbolizes fear and evil.

Snakes also have a positive spiritual symbolism. They shed their skins and therefore are seen as allegories for rebirth. The caduceus, the snake-entwined staff that symbolizes the medical profession, comes from the Greeks' belief in snakes, healing powers. In India the snake is revered as a divine symbol of enlightenment.

Fire

Fire can transform or destroy, illuminate or cause pain. Its energy is a potent symbol of eternal life or eternal damnation.

In dreams fire can mean spiritual illumination, sexual passion or change. To dream of a house burning down or a forest fire warns that you are consumed by passions. Your emotions are getting out of control and you need to calm the flames. If you are ill it can also represent a "burning" fever. Language is full of dream symbols: we describe some people as having a "fiery" temper and our "burning" desires may even spark a "flaming" argument!

Fire can also be a symbol of security. To dream of a cosy fire in the hearth indicates that you are at ease with your life, while poking the fire means arousing the passion.

As the giver of light, fire also has a spiritual side: it illuminates the darkness and is a symbol of truth. It signifies attaining a new level of understanding and leaving the old behind.

Water

Water is passive and yielding. In dreams it represents our feelings and emotions. Like the waters of the womb, it also can represent security, life and birth.

If you dream of crashing waves or rocky seas, your emotions may be out of control. A fast-flowing river or undercurrents represent emotions that are rushing ahead too fast. If the waters are peaceful then so are you.

A mysterious wide expanse symbolizes the unconscious. Like the lake in the Arthur legends, magical gifts may appear to change your life.

The cleansing qualities of water appear if you dream of bathing in clear water – there's a new start ahead. If the water is dirty or muddy you are uneasy with your feelings.

To drown in your dream shows that your emotions are overwhelming you; you need to get away from the pressures. Diving, however, symbolizes your spiritual search for life's meaning.

If you cross a river then you are crossing from one condition to another. Expect major changes in your life.

Buildings and houses

These are symbols of yourself. The upstairs represents your conscious mind and the lower floors and basement your hidden self.

If the house feels cramped this indicates frustration and a need to expand your activities or thinking. Decayed or crumbling buildings indicate that your self-image has suffered. But dreaming of a new home or a building site symbolizes positive changes in your lifestyle.

If you open doors or windows, new opportunities lie ahead.

Travel

Travelling in dreams represents the course of your life. You could be throwing off restrictions or negative attitudes by setting a new course.

The dream may tell you the direction that your life is going and how you should plan ahead. If it is a happy journey then everything is going well, but if there are obstacles or difficulties then you must beware of events or people in your life that want to stand in your way.

If you dream of missing a bus or train it shows that you are concerned about a missed opportunity.

Accidents

These are not necessarily a premonition for the future. Nightmares of this type reveal deep anxieties and fears.

A car crash may symbolize your emotional state. Are you punishing yourself? If your life feels like it's set on a course for disaster, examine your mistakes and resolve to set a new and better course

Dream symbol checklist

If you work at unravelling your own dream symbols, eventually you'll find that the images speak for themselves. In the list that follows I've also shown the similarities between dream symbols and the images found in the tarot cards. But remember — it's *your* interpretation that counts.

Adultery: Not to be interpreted too literally, these dreams usually highlight inner fears. Perhaps you have hidden worries about your sexuality or desire something that's not in your best interest.

Age: Old people may represent your higher, wiser self or even perhaps your own fears of getting older. A baby can represent your own vulnerability or in a woman the desire to have a child. Also, babies can be an allegory for a new development in your personality. Superstition tells us that to dream of a baby is an auspicious omen indicating success in everything you do.

Anchor: Do you desire security? The anchor may represent a stabilizing force. Or perhaps you feel held back in life. An old superstition states that if a girl dreams of an anchor one of her children will choose a life as a sailor.

Angel: Perhaps you've been in contact with beings from a higher astral plane, or the angel may represent your own higher transcendent self. The angel of death may be a premonition of someone dying or an indication that your attitudes must go through a death and rebirth.

Apples: In the Garden of Eden apples represented knowledge, so if religion has influenced your upbringing then this is the symbolism. Superstition says that to dream of sweet apples brings happy rewards but if they are bitter then beware of foolish mistakes.

Attic: Houses represent you. An attic may represent the things that you have excluded from your consciousness or even the higher self.

Bathing: Normally associated with cleansing, this dream may show the need to spiritually cleanse yourself or wash away unpleasant feelings. If it takes the form of a baptism then this symbolizes entering a new stage of life. If the water is dirty you may be entering a troubled period of your life.

Baldness: A fear of losing something, not necessarily your hair.

Birds: Birds are a symbol of transcendence. Consider the type of bird that your dream features. A dove may symbolize peace, a raven deceit, and a peacock pride. Symbolic dream birds found in the tarot are eagles and hawks: dominion and strength and the phoenix symbolizing renewal. Butterflies and bees have a similar symbolic meaning to birds and represent the soul in the tarot cards.

Blindness: Perhaps you're refusing to see things as they really are.

Blood: A symbol of life that recurs throughout religion. If there's blood on your hands in your dream, perhaps you feel guilty about something.

Bog: You may feel that your life is bogged down. Emotional difficulties hold you back and it's hard going at the moment.

Bridge: A transition to new things. What lies beyond? Is it a happy landscape or a foreboding one? The dream may be helping you with a difficult decision.

Burial: You may be trying to hide something. Are you hoping to get rid of some part of yourself or do you want someone out of your life? Perhaps, as they say, the past is dead and buried.

Cat: Normally associated with female qualities, the cat may symbolize the female part of yourself – your intuition maybe or your psychic self. Associated with good fortune, it could also indicate good fortune ahead. Cat symbolism appears in the tarot as well as dogs, which represent loyalty and faithfulness.

Cup: In the tarot, you will remember, cups symbolize the emotions. The holy grail, from the stories of King Arthur, symbolized the quest for higher knowledge. Your inner self may be telling you that you are embarking on a spiritual journey – a quest for the soul. A full cup may symbolize fulfilment and, if empty, it shows the need to find this spiritual self.

Church: The sacred side of you.

Clock: A symbol of time, perhaps that dates a premonition. If the clock moves backwards your life may be going in the wrong direction.

Corn: Reaping the benefits of past efforts. Shown also in the Empress of the tarot cards as a symbol for fertility and prosperity.

Door: The opening of a new area in your life.

Dancing: You feel good about your life.

Earthquake: Is your world falling apart? You may be experiencing a change of circumstances that is out of your control.

Egg: You may be "hatching new ideas" or need to "break out of your shell".

Exam: A very common dream that usually represents a fear of failure.

Fight: You may have an inner emotional conflict or you may have sensed an impending conflict with someone you know.

Fish: Fish are a universal symbol of fertility, with the promise of personal inner growth. In Christianity they symbolize Christ, who in dreams may represent your higher self. Superstition says that to dream of catching a fish means that good fortune will come your way.

Ghosts: The undiscovered side of yourself.

Gold: Gold was seen by the alchemists as representing the highest development of the human spirit. It is the reward that comes from hard work on yourself.

Hat: Your role in life. Perhaps the dream is describing your job.

Horse: A horse can represent untamed emotions or even sexual ecstasy. Horseshoes, of course, are a well-known symbol of good luck.

Hospital: Health matters need attention or maybe you need to heal an emotional problem.

Ice: You may be emotionally cold, or perhaps others are and you may need to "break the ice". Water symbolizes the emotions so you might be emotionally frozen.

Judge: This could be your conscience or it could represent the ways others see you or a conflict with authority.

Keys: A problem is answered or you will be opening a door to new horizons. Losing keys shows that you are anxious about how to solve a problem. As in tarot symbolism, keys may represent unlocking spiritual understanding.

Knife: A threat of someone harming you or even a self-destructive tendency. Freud, of course, saw knives as phallic symbols.

Ladder: Progress in spiritual or worldly status.

Lift: A shift of consciousness – upwards to spirituality or downwards into the unconscious instinctive self.

Light: Represents hope and awareness.

Marriage: The coming together of opposites and achieving inner wholeness. The bringing together of the masculine and feminine aspects of your personality.

Mirror: The mirror is your window to yourself. It shows how you feel about yourself as others see you. Do you see things as they really are, or has your mental mirror distorted the image?

Moon: The moon has always been associated with fertility and may show personal growth. As it is also associated with water, the inner growth may be linked to the emotions. If the moon is full then the circle represents the self but if it is eclipsed then you are experiencing a time of severe emotional difficulty. The moon card of the tarot expresses these things and also the psychic aspect of the enquirer's nature.

Mountains: Symbolize the spiritual quest or obstacles to be overcome – another symbol found in the tarot.

Needle: This image may show that somebody is getting on your nerves – "giving you the needle".

Night: A symbol for the unconscious, the dark side of your personality.

Owl: A symbol of wisdom that may emerge from the darkness of the unconscious.

Paradise: A symbol of the perfection that you want to achieve or even perhaps a glimpse of the afterlife.

Path: The direction you are taking in life. In the tarot, paths are often shown leading to light.

Pig: Are you being stubborn and "pig-headed"? It is also a symbol of selfishness, greed and a brutish nature.

Policeman: Your inner self is telling you to get your feelings in control. If you are arrested in your dream then you may be feeling guilty about something.

Pyramid: Pyramids and triangles pointing upwards represent the soul's search for spiritual attainment. Triangles that point downwards represent the spirit descending to matter. When two triangles interlink, as in the Star of David, it represents the harmony of heaven and earth. These same symbols recur in the tarot decks. Squares and cubes represent the earth, and circles and spheres the wholeness of the self.

Queen: Shows the motherly side of your nature or the guiding intuitive self. Similar in meaning to the High Priestess of the tarot who symbolizes female intuition.

Rain: The release of inner tension.

Rainbow: A symbol of hope. Perhaps also a bridge between the worlds. Foretells a glimpse of other worlds.

Rats: Aspects of yourself or others that probably frighten or disgust you.

Reservoir: You have more potential than you think.

Revolver: Anger or aggression may be shown by a revolver, or it could symbolize that you need to take another shot at an ambition. Guns were interpreted by Freud as sexual symbols.

Rose: A symbol of love and also a mystical image for enlightenment found in alchemy, Rosicrucianism and the tarot.

Seed: Your potential.

Sewer: An illness may be imminent or there are emotions that need to be expressed before they go stagnant.

Shadow: The unknown side of yourself. You need to become more self-aware.

Sleeping: Shows aspects of yourself that have not as yet become part of your conscious awareness but you are aware of the need to awaken these things in yourself.

Spider: Distrust of others.

Storm: An inner conflict that is overwhelming you. You need to be more calm about things.

Sword: In the tarot these are a symbol of the will and also of strife. In dreams they have a similar meaning. Can also be a Freudian phallic symbol or symbolize power, honour or war.

Teacher: You need to study or are being taught life's difficult lessons.

Tower: Your dream symbol may, as in the tarot cards, use a tower as a symbol of the spirit rising above material troubles.

Train: The direction of your life at the moment. If you miss a train, you may fear missing an opportunity.

Tree: Trees are one of the oldest religious symbols, representing life. The type of tree says a lot about how you feel about your life. Does it bear fruit? Is it strong like the oak or rotten, withered and battered? Trees are strong yet they can bend with the wind –

perhaps you should do the same when faced with adversity.

Unicorn: Superstition says that it is unlucky to dream of a unicorn as it means that someone will trouble you. In alchemy, however, it is seen as a transcendent spiritual symbol of power and purity.

Veil: Something hidden from yourself or others.

Violence: You may be repressing your feelings that now have found an outlet in your dreams. Take violent dreams as an impetus to express your emotions in a natural, gentle way.

Water lily: A symbol of enlightenment.

Wedding: Superstition says that to dream of a wedding symbolizes a death. A more sensible interpretation is that it represents the coming together of different ideas. If you feel troubled in the dream you may have worries about your own marriage.

X-ray: You may be worried about your health or it can symbolize the ability to see through a problem.

Yourself: To see yourself in a dream may show that you are able to understand yourself from another's viewpoint. Also it could show the beginnings of learning astral travel.

Zebra: Superstition says that to dream of a zebra brings bad luck but, like every dream symbol there's more than one interpretation: perhaps, like the stripes of its skin, you only see things in black and white.

Daydreaming exercise

If you have real problems unravelling a dream's symbolism, put a little time aside later in the day and drift into a daydream. At first this may be difficult, particularly if you feel wide-awake but with practice you can turn it into an art. Daydreaming helps you get to the bottom of what a dream means because as you do so the images from the night before will reappear and your conscious mind can now work with and even influence the imagery.

Ever since our school days we've been told that daydreaming is bad. But it's not: it's a powerful creative tool. Charles Dickens wrote most of his best work after a period of light reverie. Mozart, Napoleon, Edison, Churchill and Margaret Thatcher were all known to catnap to solve problems or restore their drive — they all slept less than five hours a night.

A light catnap for five minutes will restore your body and stimulate energy. Try it. Drift into a light sleep during the day and watch the images passing through your head. Many will relate to the dream you wrote down. Your subconscious is still working on the problem you set it and adding new ideas gathered during the day. Or you can focus on a new problem for a quick answer to a job you're working on.

Just use the same techniques as before. Set a question, watch the imagery, interpret it and put the answer into action. In addition, you will find that working with your subconscious in this way will greatly increase the clairvoyant abilities that will emerge in a symbolic way during your reverie.

We only use about 10 per cent of our brain in our waking life. By calling upon the powers of the subconscious mind you open up all sorts of new possibilities. Use it. Not only will you solve your problems — you may even become a genius!

Lucid dreams

If you can master daydreaming, and remain semi-conscious while sleeping lightly, or if you have had a hypnagogic dream, you will soon be able to progress to an incredibly interesting dream activity: lucid dreaming. These are extremely vivid dreams that unlock a whole new world of psychic experience.

Most of the time we don't realize that we've been dreaming until we've woken up. It is possible, however, during deep sleep, to become conscious that we're dreaming while the dream is in progress. Researchers call these lucid dreams and they can be directed much like a director directs a film.

Sounds difficult? Over the last 50 years researchers have developed a series of simple lucid dream techniques that they claim anyone can master. By using these methods we can draw upon the powerful creative forces of the unconscious. The mind is a powerful computer that we can use to solve our problems.

The value of lucid dreaming is enormous. Dream subjects report that their creative abilities are increased, they become more aware of their life goals and their self-confidence is increased. There is an understanding that it is possible to control their personal destiny.

Lucid dreaming builds a bridge between the conscious and unconscious. Like any skill it takes effort to learn at first but it becomes easier, and in time, effortless.

Lucid dreams

1 You must prepare yourself the day before. Clearly you're not dreaming when awake, but occasionally stop your daily tasks and ask yourself, "Am I dreaming?" This will establish a habit during the day that you can carry into your sleeping hours.

2 Before going to sleep that night, tell yourself, "I will 'wake-up' in my dream and *know* that I am dreaming." Once you've programmed the instructions, you will, in time, have a lucid dream. This means that you will learn to change the dream while it is in progress. If, for example, you regularly dream of being chased you can now change the dream and chase the pursuer. You take control.

3 If an ordinary dream wakes you in the night, you can start changing it into a lucid dream. Carefully review it in your mind and write it down if you like, but don't worry about interpretations at this stage.

4 As you go back to sleep let the dream rerun through your mind but this time change it very slightly. Add another character or event that wasn't there in the first dream. By doing this you gradually learn to influence and change dreams. With effort you will gradually be able to create your own dream landscapes, characters and events the ultimate wish-fulfilment.

Out-of-body dreams

Advances in medical technology have enabled doctors to resuscitate patients that would otherwise have died, and some of them report very strange stories indeed. Although for a short time clinically brain-dead, these patients have described seeing the operating theatre's proceedings from a vantage point on the ceiling. They travelled out of their bodies!

Some of the most interesting studies were of blind patients who correctly reported the colours and designs of the clothes worn by their surgeons. Some were even able to give the exact readings on the anaesthetists' machinery.

In dreams it is possible to do the same without any danger to our health. Psychics call this "astral travelling" and in the East it has been known for centuries as "Cloud Walking". The American Indians believed the same.

Psychics believe that we all have a duplicate etheric body. This is an exact copy of our physical body and survives death. When we sleep this astral duplicate sometimes goes on night jaunts. Using simple techniques it is possible to release yourself from the physical body and really fly in your dreams.

Astral travel

1 Before dropping off to sleep, put your body into a deep state of relaxation. Do this by systematically tensing and releasing each muscle one at a time. Start with the toes and work up the body to the face. This will put your body into such an unfamiliar deep state of relaxation that in the early days you may feel a little discomfort. Your body may feel unbearably heavy but there's nothing to worry about.

2 Now let your breathing become slow and deep – you may want to use some of the breathing techniques we learnt at the beginning of the book. Slow, deep breathing will relax you further and keep you alert. Focus your attention on the centre of your forehead but *don't* fall asleep.

3 Become aware of just how heavy your body feels. Think of it as being cumbersome and made of clay. Now set your attention on your astral duplicate body. See it as made of light. It is weightless and free. Picture in your mind's eye images of bubbles, sunlight, feathers floating on the breeze, smoke rising upwards. Your body is heavy but the soul is weightless.

4 At this point many people report of being able to "see" the darkened room even though their eyes are closed. It appears to be bathed in a purple light. If you get this far, try to focus your attention on the ceiling light fitting.

5 Imagine drawing the light bulb towards you. As you do this you may feel yourself floating upward towards the ceiling. Try to remain conscious. You will become aware of floating in your astral self and may even see your sleeping body laid below you on the bed.

Astral worlds

The material world is only one of many planes of existence. When you undertake astral travelling you may decide to visit places on the earth plane – go and have a free holiday at the great pyramid or have a glimpse of tomorrow's exam papers. But there are other realms that can be explored in the astral body and, some say, other beings and species to be encountered.

When, as a teenager, I had my first experience of out-of-body travel, I was so shocked to see my body laid on the bed that I panicked. The result was that I re-entered my body like a whip lash. I saw a flash of brilliant white light and there was a loud bang as if a gun had fired off next to my ears. I awoke drenched in cold sweat.

Astral travelling is quite safe but it's uncomfortable if you return to the body too quickly. It happened to me without ever having heard about the phenomena, so naturally I panicked – I thought I was dead!

If you want to return to your body, just think of it and you'll return gently and naturally. If you retain peace of mind you'll never need experience an uncomfortable re-entry. Getting back into the body is easy. It's getting out that takes the real effort.

STRANGE PSYCHIC STORIES OF THE STARS

Kirk Douglas

In 1991, film star Kirk Douglas suffered serious injuries in a helicopter crash after it was in collision with a light aircraft in California. Douglas received serious back and head injuries and was fighting for his life. He experienced what doctors call a NDE (Near Death Experience) and for a short time left his physical body.

"It was like I was suspended in space," he said. "There was no concept of time. I saw the most vivid coloured lights. It was like a most glorious tunnel of life".

He added, "There was never a moment I was as close to God as I was then. I will never take life, things or people for granted again. I'm more appreciative of being able to open my eyes in the morning and see those I love close by."

(PN 13/4/91)

Dream meetings

Have you ever said the same thing as someone at the same time or known who's at the other end of the phone the moment it rings? You are experiencing telepathy — the ability to communicate thoughts. We have spoken to many people and received many letters from people who claim to have had the exact same dream on the same night. Some could be explained as coincidence (you have read about common dreams) but others defy traditional explanations.

People who believe in reincarnation believe that these dreams are a recall of a shared past life. There have been many fascinating instances of people who have dreamed of another time in history, and careful research has proved them to be right.

Of all the psychic skills telepathy is the most well proved. When our conscious mind relaxes in sleep, our psychic abilities are at their peak. And in dreams we can communicate our inner thoughts to people we know.

Perhaps there's something we want to say but haven't the courage to voice. So the unconscious finds a route for us. We communicate with one another through our dreams.

Dream telepathy

1 You will need to ask a friend to help you with this one. Ask them to concentrate on a 15-minute segment of video before they go to sleep. (Moving images have been proved superior to static pictures in laboratory tests of telepathy.) Make sure it's a film you've never seen.

2 As you fall asleep use the lucid dream techniques already described to stimulate a controlled dream. Ask your friend to do the same. You must both command yourselves to dream about the video. If you "wake up" in your dream, scan the terrain for the video messages.

3 Next morning note carefully all the images that you dreamed of the night before. Include every possible detail no matter how irrelevant they

may seem. Note also your feelings, thoughts and impressions.

4 Once you have recorded your notes you and your friend should get together as soon as possible. Watch the video clip together and compare it to your notes. Are there any similarities? You may both be surprised at the number of correct targets.

Working in this way utilizes all the dream skills you have now studied: telepathy, astral travel, symbolism and lucid dreaming. Conducting experiments with a friend or group of friends goes a long way to proving that the techniques we are using are not fantasy – they are a reality that we can prove together.

Another interesting experiment is to arrange a 'drean conference' with a group of friends. Arrange to 'meet' in your dreams at a landmark you all know. Later you can compare notes about the things seen and said when you saw the target place.

Some famous dreamers

The Chinese philosopher Chuang Chou dreamed he was a butterfly. The dream was so vivid that when he awoke he couldn't decide if he was a man dreaming of being a butterfly or a butterfly dreaming of being a man.

Whether you're solving the great mysteries of existence or trying to decide which clothes to wear, dreams continue solving problems as you sleep. They are a tremendous source of creativity and have inspired philosophers, artists and scientists alike.

Wordsworth's greatest poems, he said, were inspired by dreams, as was "Kubla Khan" by Colridge. Jules Verne, Charles Dickens and Robert Louis Stevenson were all influenced by dreams. And the characters in Jane Eyre were spun from the dreams of Charlotte Brontë.

Many scientific advances also owe their inception to dreams. The famous physicist Niels Bohr was trying to understand the nature of the atom. One night he dreamed of a sun composed of burning gases with planets orbiting it attached by fine threads. When he awoke he realized that this was the solution to his puzzle. It explained the structure of the atom and heralded the birth of atomic physics.

Even the sewing machine owes its invention to a dream. Elias Howe was stumped for a solution for a working model. But a dream brought the answer: Howe dreamed that a savage king ordered him to invent a sewing machine. When Howe said he couldn't, the tribe raised their spears to kill him. Then Howe noticed that each spear had a hole in it just above the point. This was the vital clue needed for the commercial perfection of the sewing machine.

Dreams also contained prophecies. As a young man, Oliver Cromwell had a dream in which a huge female figure drew back the curtains around his bed. She told him that he would be the greatest man in England – but not the king. The impossible came true.

Queen Marie Antoinette dreamed of a glowing red sun rising above a temple pillar that cracked and fell to the ground. She understood it to represent her fall from power. Abraham Lincoln also saw his impending doom. He is said to have dreamed of his assassination and of his body lying in state.

STRANGE PSYCHIC STORIES OF THE STARS

Joseph Stalin

Who would have thought that the Communist leader of Russia would be interested in psychics? Few people realize that Joseph Stalin was interested in spiritual matters, but he once studied for the priesthood in the Titlis theological seminary.

When he heard of the astonishing psychic abilities of the Polish Jew Wolf Messing he decided to meet him. The perplexed Messing was arrested and questioned by Stalin himself about the destiny of Russia.

Stalin decided to put Messing to the test. He was to undertake a "psychic bank robbery" and take 100 000 roubles from the Moscow Gosbank, where he was unknown.

Wolf Messing used his telepathically projected hypnotic powers. He walked into the bank and handed the cashier a blank sheet of paper who responded by giving Messing exactly 100 000 roubles. Two of Stalin's official witnesses confirmed to their leader what had happened. When the cashier realized that he was holding a blank sheet of paper he fainted from shock.

As if this wasn't enough, Stalin demanded that Messing undertake another impossible task. He took Messing to a secure Government building and personally ordered three sets of guards to ensure that Messing did not leave the building. Messing succeeded again, cheekily waving goodbye to a high government official looking out of one of the windows.

But Stalin still wasn't satisfied. Messing must risk his life again. He was ordered to illegally enter Stalin's heavily guarded country house. Messing used mental suggestion to convince the guards and servants that he was really Lavrenti Beria, the head of the secret police, even though there was no physical resemblance. Once again he triumphed.

Strangest of all is the dream of the author Mark Twain. During the 1850s he worked the Mississippi river boats together with his brother Henry. Mark Twain dreamed that his brother died – Henry was in a metal coffin resting on two chairs, and a bouquet with a single crimson flower at its centre had been placed on his chest.

A few weeks later Henry died when the *Pennsylvania's* boilers exploded. The dead crew were placed in wooden coffins. Only Henry had a metal coffin – but there was no bouquet, Mark noted when he looked at his brother. As he stood there a woman entered the room and placed a bouquet of white flowers on Henry's chest. At its centre was a single red rose.

Chapter 10

Group work

A problem shared is a problem halved and a joy shared is a joy doubled

This is a unique period of human history: a time of danger but also a time when the inner beauty of man will bud and bloom. We will never solve the terrible problems of the 20th century by politics and money. The impetus towards Utopia must come from within. Change ourselves and the world will change also. And it's happening now.

The age of Aquarius

The earth is like a gigantic gyroscope which orients itself at a particular angle even though it is hurtling through space in its orbit around the sun. The earth also wobbles slightly on its axis and this creates what astrologers call "the precession of the equinoxes".

The vernal (spring) equinox is the point where the sun passes the equator moving from south to north and is designated nought degrees Aries. Over a period of about 2120 years the vernal equinox moves through a zodiac sign. At present it is on the border between the constellations of Pisces and Aquarius. The much talked about "Age of Aquarius" begins when the pointer fully enters the sign of Aquarius.

Eastern astrology believes that we entered a new and better age in 1700. Kali Yuga, the repressive age of iron, gave way to Dwapara Yuga, the age of electrical and atomic energy. Dwapara Yuga lasts 24 000 years and is considered more auspicious for spiritual growth.

The qualities of Aquarius and Dwapara Yuga herald a time of great scientific advancement. Also, the Aquarian traits of individuality, communication, humanitarianism and spirituality will dominate the world consciousness. It means that people will be searching spiritually, both as individuals and collectively.

Already the Aquarian influence is being felt. Psychic and spiritual movements are flowering all over the world and have loosely been called "the New Age movement". Like the Aquarian character, they are innovative and highly individual organizations. The emphasis is on finding your own path to truth. Doctrine and creed are frowned upon. Instead of seeing God as a being separate to man, God becomes something to find within yourself. The Celestial Road leads straight to your own heart. And there are millions of people already walking it.

Working together

Psychic, healing and meditative powers quicken when a group of people sit together with a common objective. Jane and I have visited many small groups, of about six to ten people, who are seeking spiritually. Group meditation is common to most. Healing thoughts are sent out to individuals or to the planet earth. Members talk about their own experiences and spiritual quest. Sometimes dreams are discussed. Often crystals, oracles or Tibetan bells are introduced. Outings are arranged to visit Spiritual places or organizations. There's no rigid, set format. Experiment is the keynote.

Many sit with the primary objective of raising consciousness. If someone wants to introduce an idea they've perhaps seen elsewhere or wants to suggest a meditation experiment, they are encouraged to contribute. The best groups are flexible — a place where you can learn from others and also from yourself. A creative atmosphere is the key.

Researchers have established that many clairvoyants come from artistic backgrounds. Creativity and psychic gifts are complementary to each other.

Bring out a person's creativity and the psychic gifts are encouraged.

Bright colour and symbolism are also conducive to expanded consciousness. Why not start by transforming a spare room into a sanctuary? Fill it with colour and imagery: posters, paintings, plants, cushions, drapes, subtle lighting, incense, music, chimes, murals, crystal glass, mandalas — I know one group that saved to build a fountain in their sanctuary. Be just as bold and imaginative.

Make your group inspiring and exciting. Charge a fee. Set goals for the funds raised to expand the sanctuary, perhaps even to, one day, buy or rent a special building. Everyone will enjoy this expanding process.

Group structure

Even the most spiritual of groups needs a structure. Many are run by fully developed mediums but this is not strictly necessary. Certainly it's helpful to invite various psychic specialists and mediums to teach you their skills but everyone can take a turn being the group leader. In my own circle everyone gets a chance to control at least one aspect of the proceedings.

A group should sit in a circle. There should be an ample supply of water to drink between psychic links. A small coffee table in the centre is useful on which to place cards, crystals or objects for psychometry. There's no need for complete darkness but subdued lighting or a red or blue bulb is preferable for developing auric sight or mediumship.

This is the structure I use for my own group:

Opening the circle

1. **Opening:** One member opens with either a prayer or a positive affirmation. We ask that the spirit helpers from the higher planes draw close to us to protect and teach us.

2. **Breathing:** About five minutes is dedicated to breathing exercises with the objective of increasing prana and stilling the mind.

3. **Opening the aura:** The group leader for the evening talks the others

through the technique of opening the aura and raising the light through the chakras (see Chapter 3).

4. **Meditation:** This is usually done in silence so that people can attune themselves with their spirit helpers. Sometimes a member of the group will talk the others through a visualization. In the early stages, the meditation lasts only a few minutes and is increased as the aspirants learn to sit.

5. **Talking:** Each takes a turn describing briefly what they felt during the meditation: the images and symbolism and if they felt their spirit guides draw close. Verbalizing your experiences is helpful in integrating your experience.

6. **Development and experiment:** The majority of the session is devoted to practising the psychic skills outlined in this book. In the early months a great deal of time is dedicated to developing psychometry, as in my opinion this is the bedrock of psychic development. Sometimes sitters are asked to bring objects and photographs from people other than themselves, and guests are invited to practise on them.

A theme is agreed for some weeks: Dowsing, Crystals, Zener Cards, Dreams, Tarot, Sand Reading, etc. All the skills you've read about are great fun to practise together. Also, in my own group, we occasionally chant the mantra Om — it lifts the vibrations considerably.

Working together increases your self-confidence and provides a well of psychic energy that you can draw from.

Gradually a spiritual bond develops between the sitters. It usually takes a few months before the group becomes finalized. Some may leave and new seekers may join. Once the circle is firmly established, a tremendous loving power is felt within the room. The members want everyone to progress and there are no petty jealousies. Create these conditions and you'll have tremendous success.

When the energy feels right the group can progress to mediumistic development. Each person can take a turn linking with another member's aura and gradually progressing from a psychic reading to a mediumistic one.

Closing the circle

1. **Absent healing:** When you've finished practising, the spiritual energy that's been generated can be used for absent healing. Everyone closes their eyes and one of the circle talks the others through a visualization. Each person in turn names those people they would like healing to be sent to and the speaker talks the group through a visualization

2. **Closing the aura:** A circle member talks the group through the closing of the aura and chakras. During the meeting it is important that the circle is not broken by someone leaving to use the toilet, hurrying off to catch a bus, etc. Always make sure that every member pays strict attention to the process of closing down.

3. **Closing:** When everyone is back to normal consciousness a prayer or a word of thanks to the spirit is said.

4. **Tea and biscuits:** Save the chit-chat till now. You'll all have loads to talk about after the circle.

Other group experiments

Here are a few ideas that can only be practised as a group:

Psychic experiment

Envelope game

You will, no doubt, want to develop your psychometry skills at your meetings. Once you start getting good results, try this interesting experiment. It's a bit like the children's game "Consequences".

1 Before the meeting starts, each person is given a large envelope and a pen. They write their name on the inside of the flap and fold it into the envelope. The sitters place the envelopes on their lap through the

meditation and opening procedure.

2 Afterwards the envelopes are returned to the circle leader and shuffled. They have absorbed the individual vibrations of the sitters and can be used for a psychometry experiment.

William Lyon Mackenzie King

It caused a sensation in Canada when the public discovered in 1950 that their former Prime Minister, who held office from 1935 till 1948, regularly consulted with the dead. Mackenzie King made no secret about this to his intimate friends, some of whom joined his seances in his library at home. King used both the crystal ball and a ouija board and his diaries reveal he experienced visions and prophetic dreams.

3 An envelope is handed out to each person. They are asked to use psychometry to pick up the impressions they feel. Each person should write a couple of sentences about their impressions at the top of the envelope then fold it backwards. Each envelope is then passed to the person on the left to do the same again.

4 When the envelopes have gone full circle, they are returned to the evening's group leader and the flaps lifted. Each is then given back to the original person that held it during meditation.

5 Reading your envelope is intriguing. Not only do you have a psychometry reading from everyone in the group but you see your own notes about the way you feel about yourself.

Psychic experiment

Blindfold clairvoyance

One of the arguments against mediumship or psychic reading is that the psychic unconsciously reads subtle psychological signals such as facial expressions, body language or the vocal clues of the sitter. This next experiment proves the sceptics wrong.

1 Place two chairs facing each other in the centre of the circle. Sit one of the members in a chair and blindfold them. Select another person to sit in the chair opposite. Now all shuffle around a little so that the blindfolded person has no idea who's sitting opposite them.

2 The blindfolded psychic should then make a psychic profile for the person in front of them. The sitter answers with a nod or shake of the head for yes or no and the group leader says aloud what answer is being given. Afterwards the blindfold is removed and the contact can be discussed in more detail.

This type of practice greatly reinforces your realization that psychic gifts are not determined by visual or auditory clues from the sitter.

Psychic experiment

Levitation

Try this simple levitation experiment, involving willed concentration.

1 One person sits in a chair while four others try to lift him by placing their index fingers under his knees and arms. It's impossible, of course. The four people then place their hands on top of his head in a pile (just like in the children's game Pat-a-cake Pat-a-cake).

2 The next step is for everyone, particularly the subject himself, to visualize that the subject is getting lighter. The group leader should encourage this by talking the others through: "The subject is getting lighter and lighter. You can all sense him/her wanting to rise from the chair. Imagine light, light bubbles floating in the breeze. You see feathers floating in the air, rising, rising upward to touch the heavens. See smoke gently rising to the sky. You feel light. Your body is weightless. You are like a dandelion seed tossed by the wind. You are as light as a cloud, free as a bird." You don't have to use these exact words. Use your own imagination to create a visualized scenario that encourages everyone to think about the subject getting lighter.

3 At a signal from the group leader everyone removes their hands and tries again to lift the subject with only their index fingers. This time the seated person rises effortlessly into the air!

Nobody can adequately explain just why this experiment works. Some believe that there's a physical explanation, while spoon-bending psychics, like Uri Geller, believe that paranormal powers are involved.

Belief in the possibility of this experiment working seems to help. Children, who have fewer preconceptions about the impossible, seem to get the most interesting results. If it doesn't work first time with the adults get the kids to have a try.

STRANGE PSYCHIC STORIES OF THE STARS

Winston Churchill

Sir Winston Churchill, the man of destiny who guided Britain through World War II, possessed a natural psychic gift that saved his life many times. He was a visionary. Every prophecy he made in the 1930s was fulfilled, said Baroness Asquith.

During the Boer War, as a reporter for the *Morning Post,* his train was ambushed and he was confined to a prison camp. He escaped into territory unknown to him. His intuition guided him to knock at the door of a house and recklessly reveal that he was British. "Thank God you have come here," cried the stranger. "It is the only house where you would not have been handed over. We are all British here."

His life was saved again when fighting during World War I on the Western Front. One day, while he was with the General, his dugout was blown up. He said later, "And then there came the sensation that a hand had been stretched out to move me in the nick of time from a fatal spot."

Churchill's psychic gift saved him again during the Blitz. He always sat in the nearside car seat but on this occasion insisted on sitting in the back. A bomb landed close by which would have killed him if he hadn't made this impulsive decision. When his wife asked him why he had not used his normal seat he said, "Something said to me 'Stop' before I reached the car door held open for me. It then appeared to me I was told I was meant to open the other side and get in and sit there – and that's what I did."

In 1940 Churchill again sensed danger and "saw" the huge windows at Horse Guards Parade, which backs onto 10 Downing Street, being smashed. He ushered everyone to safety three minutes before splintered glass sprayed the building.

Churchill believed in destiny and that some invisible power guided his life. "I have the feeling that we had a Guardian because we serve a great cause," he explained, "and that we shall have that Guardian so long as we serve that cause faithfully."

Chapter 11

A Code of Conduct

Are you psychic?

When you asked yourself this question at the beginning of the book you probably weren't sure. If you've studied the exercises and practised the techniques by now you may have discovered that you're a lot more psychic than you at first thought. The modern world, stuck in its materialism, needs good, spiritual psychics more than ever. But it can do without the charlatans and frauds — and there are a few. Many professional psychics are sincere in their work but some don't have a real psychic gift. It's all too easy to buy a set of tarot cards, learn the meanings and start giving readings.

I've tried to show you the psychic skills that underpin the use of oracles: the importance of meditation, tuning in to vibration and using your psychic intuition. Never become smug — keep pushing yourself and try to make every reading the best you've ever done. This book has put you on the first rungs of the ladder. It's just been a taster and now you can progress by studying more specialist books or taking part in workshops. But I hope that it's given you an insight into what the psychic gift is all about and how it applies to the many methods of clairvoyance. If your motives are right you won't go far wrong.

Above all, be honest. Some psychics have huge, very unspiritual egos. Their outrageous advertisements say it all: "Madam Za Za sees all, knows all, and will solve your marriage, work, luck and any problem you have. Come and see the world's top international clairvoyant as sought out by celebrities." Rubbish. Their only international claim to fame may be that they gave a reading to someone while on holiday in Spain. Most celebrities are reclusive people who hardly want to have their photograph displayed on a seaside clairvoyant's sign. In fact, the photos of celebrities dotted around their room are usually bogus.

Other clairvoyants are completely out-of-line. They get carried away with fantasy about reincarnation and spirit guides and are away with the elves and fairies. They specialize in telling you things for which there's no empirical proof. One so-called "Celtic Medium" (whatever that means) slipped into a trance and spouted utter rubbish to me for an hour. When she "awoke" she demanded three times her fee because the reading had gone over her usual time. God only knows what damage this woman could do to severely bereaved or emotionally desperate people. Needless to say, her liberal quantity of predictions never came to pass.

Problems with people

❖ If you want to use your psychic gifts to help people, you'd best ask yourself some serious questions to see if you're ready:

❖ What would you say to a person who knew they were suffering from a terminal illness?

❖ How would you comfort someone who's severely bereaved?

❖ What would you do if partway through your reading you realized the sitter suffered from a severe psychiatric problem? And how would you stop them pestering you if they became infatuated with you?

❖ Could you deal with a poltergeist or a haunting?

❖ Supposing your sitter is seriously contemplating suicide, what would you do?

Hopefully, you'll never encounter some of the more extreme cases but you must prepare yourself. Don't expect everyone's problems to be simple and easy to solve. Some people turn to a clairvoyant as a last resort, when counselling or psychiatric therapy has failed them.

A good way to veto people is to work only through personal recommendation or with people you know. *You will need a great deal more experience behind you before you can work with the general public.* I would also recommend that all clairvoyants, no matter how long they've been at it, learn the basics of psychology or take a course in counselling. And just as a healer should never suggest stopping medication or seeing the doctor, you must not interfere in the painstaking work of psychiatrists.

Peter Clark, the ex-presenter of TV's "Crimewatch", is now a full-time journalist for the national papers. He interviewed Jane and myself for an article about how people had been helped or harmed by seeing a clairvoyant. Like any good journalist, he wanted to take an unbiased view and state both sides of the case. In the article we called for a code of conduct that all psychics should abide by.

The don'ts

❖ **Don't predict a death.** A genuine psychic will know that this is impossible. It is not something that we have clairvoyant access to.

❖ **Don't play doctor.** Under no circumstances suggest someone should go against their doctor's advice.

❖ **Don't be the guru.** Stress that you are only an ordinary person or the sitter may think that you're the only person in the world that can solve their problems. (Psychiatrists call this transference.)

❖ **Don't make exaggerated claims.** You can't guarantee that you can mediumistically communicate with the person that they want to hear from in spirit. Nor can you guarantee to solve their problems.

❖ **Don't embellish clairvoyance.** Keep your evidence clear. If you dry up, stop the sitting. It's no good adding a load of junk from your own subconscious to the reading.

❖ **Don't force yourself on people.** There's nothing worse than the over-eager psychic that pushes clairvoyance onto people while waiting for a bus, for instance. Some people just aren't ready yet to hear from their long-dead grandad.

STRANGE PSYCHIC STORIES OF THE STARS

Mae West

Although I never met direct voice medium Leslie Flint, I have spoken to many of his sitters who have testified to his accuracy. One of his clients was Hollywood legend Mae West. At one of his seances Mae made contact with her dead brother – he gave the pet name "Diamond Kelly". The medium's close colleague Bram Rogers said, "She was happy with the results. Later she sang two of her show numbers for us. It was an enchanting evening with a monumental Hollywood personality."

(PN 26/12/87)

But Mae West was very psychic herself. According to author Danton Walker, in his book, *Spooks Delux*, Mae said of a well-known Los Angeles clairvoyant: "She taught me to go 'into the silence' 'how to blank my consciousness and let the inner voice come through. I then became aware that to some extent I had been doing this all my life. I remember once sitting at a prizefight and having the entire plot of a play come to me, out of nowhere."

(quoted from Amazing psychic experiences of the famous-Julie Byron Page 206)

She also sat for psychic development with US medium John Kelly after she saw her friend receive accurate evidence of survival. "Some of the things he told us at the meeting were astonishing, things about which he could not possibly know in advance."

(PN issue 2955)

In 1970 Miss West told the *Sunday Times Magazine* that she clairvoyantly saw crowds of individuals "like a montage". Describing herself as "a very normal, healthy person," she continued, "I don't imagine things and hear voices. I know something exists around me."

(PN issue 2955)

A month before she died, Mae West received a message during a seance in her Hollywood apartment. It was from her old friend, actor Clifton Webb. She was told that they were expecting her.

The dos

❖ **Instil optimism.**   Try to see beyond the bad events to better times. Of course there may be obstacles ahead but help the person realize the power of positive thinking. You're a useless clairvoyant if you only breed despair.

❖ **Stress free will.**   A prediction that inhibits a person's spiritual growth is worthless. If, for example, you said to a young girl, "Your marriages will all end in divorce," they probably would. How could a marriage last if they're subconsciously thinking that it's doomed? Clients may remember things they've been told for the rest of their lives.

❖ **Give evidence.**   Try to give quantifiable facts about the sitter's life or those they know in spirit. Don't talk only about woolly future events.

❖ **Cultivate spiritual values.**   Make your daily life part of your psychic work. Try to change your attitudes and develop spiritual good habits.

❖ **Be good-humoured.**   Try to spread a little happiness with your psychic work.

❖ **Improve yourself.**   Psychic development is a lifelong process. Like an artist that's never fully satisfied with their latest painting, always try to improve on the quality of your evidence.

Progressing Further

This book had taken you through the first few steps toward full psychic development. The skills you've learnt may act as an impetus towards further progress. Mediumship (spirit communication) may be your next goal but it will take another book to explain the safe development of these skills. For serious students, who are eager to progress further, I've included on pages 182-183 a list of contact addresses to guide you in the right direction.

YOUR ZENER CARDS

Printed on the next few pages are 25 Zener cards that you can cut out and use in your psychic experiments. It is not practical to print them in colour so we suggest that you use coloured pencils or felt tip pens to do this. Also, it is suggested that you glue the paper to light cardboard with a plain back to make them more durable.

CROSSES: bright red

WAVY LINES: light blue

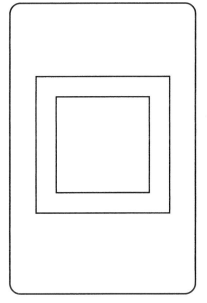

SQUARES: black

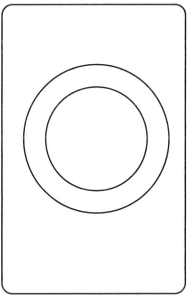

CIRCLES: bright orange

STARS: light green

CROSSES: bright red

WAVY LINES: light blue

SQUARES: black

CIRCLES: bright orange

STARS: light green

CROSSES: bright red

WAVY LINES: light blue

SQUARES: black

CIRCLES: bright orange

STARS: light green

CROSSES: bright red

WAVY LINES: light blue

SQUARES: black

CIRCLES: bright orange

STARS: light green

CROSSES: bright red

WAVY LINES: light blue

SQUARES: black

CIRCLES: bright orange

STARS: light green

Useful Addresses

Readers are welcome to write to Craig and Jane care of the publishers. They would particularly like to hear about unusual paranormal stories that they may research and include in their future books. Please include a stamped, self-addressed envelope.

PSYCHIC, MEDIUMISTIC AND HEALING DEVELOPMENT

SPIRITUALISM
The world's biggest teaching headquarters for developing mediums
The Arthur Findlay College, Stanstead Hall, Stanstead, Mountfitchet, Essex, CM24 8UD

SPIRITUALIST ASSOCIATION OF GREAT BRITIAN (SAGB)
Daily public demonstrations of mediumship, with private sittings and workshops available with qualified mediums
The Spiritualist Association of Great Britain, Belgrave Square, London.

THE GREATER WORLD
Mediumistic teachings for those with Christian beliefs
The Greater World, 3-5 Conway Street, London WIP 5HA

PHYSICAL MEDIUMSHIP
The development and promotion of physical mediumistic phenomena
The Noah's Ark Society, "Treetops"
Hall Road, Cromer, Norfolk NR27 9JQ

WHITE EAGLE
A worldwide organization based on the mediumship of Grace Cook
White Eagle Lodge, New Lands, Brewells Lane, Liss, Hampshire GU33 7HY

HEALING
It's best to get a thorough training if you want to heal. The National Federation of Spiritual Healers (NFSH) is a healing organization that is now recommended by many GPs.
National Federation of Spiritual Healers, Old Manor Farm Studio, Church Street, Sunbury-on-Thames, Middlesex TW16 6RG

HARRY EDWARDS
Harry Edwards was a wonderful healer. Advice and help can be obtained from the organization that continues to heal in his name
The Harry Edwards Spiritual Healing Sanctuary Trust, Burrows Lea, Shere, Guildford, Surrey GU5 9QG

REIKI HEALING Japanese spiritual healing workshops
The Association of European Reiki Practitioners, 8 Ashmore Road, Cotteridge, Birmingham B30 2HA

MEDICAL DOWSING
Lectures and courses on using dowsing to treat illness
British Society of Dowsers, Sycamore Barn, Hastingleigh, Ashford, Kent TN25 5HW

PSYCHIC SCIENCE AND PHILOSOPHY

SOCIETY OF PSYCHICAL RESEARCH
Worldwide scientific investigators of psychic phenomena
Society of Psychical Research, 49 Marloes Road, London, W8 6LA

EDGAR CAYCE
A huge library and information source to promote an understanding of the work of America's most famous psychic.
The Association for Research and Enlightenment, PO Box 595, Virginia Beach, VA 23451, USA
The Edgar Cayce Centre, PO Box 8, Stanley, County Durham DH9 7XQ

THEOSOPHY
Philosophical teachings initiated by the trance mediumship of Madam Blavatsky
The Blavatsky Trust, Avalon, Little Weston, Sparkford, Yeovil BA22 7HP

ANTHROPOSOPHY
Spiritual teachings and weekend workshops based on the philosophy of Rudolf Steiner
Rudolph Steiner House, 35 Park Road, London NW1 6XT

PSYCHIC NEWS PAPERS
There are many good papers and magazines about psychic and mediumistic development. If you want to keep abreast of what's going on, read this interesting weekly newspaper (available in the USA & Australia by mail order).
Psychic News, 2 Tavistock Chambers, Bloomsbury Way, London WC1A 2SE
Fate Magazine, PO Box 64383, St Paul, MN 55164-0383, USA

"NEW AGE" GROUPS

FOUNTAIN INTERNATIONAL
An organization that hopes to improve the world through meditation, crystals and spiritual awareness.
Fountain International, 35 Padacre Road, Torquay, Devon TQ2 8PX

FINDHORN
Workshops and courses available that teach about meditation, consciousness and Devas (nature spirits).
Findhorn Foundation, The Park, Forres, Scotland IV36 OTS

MEDITATION AND YOGA

YOGA
Develop your meditation, breathing and physical fitness.
British Wheel of Yoga, 1 Hamilton Place, Boston Road, Sleaford, Lincs NG34 7ES

TIBETAN MEDITATION RETREAT
Kagyu Samye Ling Tibetan Centre, Eskdalemuir, Langholm, Dumfriesshire, Scotland DG13 OQL
SAI BABA Details available about this Eastern guru from :
Peggy Mason, The Lodge, 10 Broadwater Down, Tunbridge Wells, Kent TN2 5NG

YOGANANDA
An international meditation society based on the Kiri Yoga teachings of Paramahansa Yogananda
Self-Realization Fellowship, 3880 San Rafael Ave Los Angeles, California 90065 USA

TRANSCENDENTAL MEDITATION
Mantra meditation techniques based on the teachings of Maharishi Mahesh Yogi.
Transcendental Meditation, Freepost, London SW1P 4YY

Glossary

astral body The subtle body of light that encases the physical body. In sleep it can separate from the physical body.

astral travel Travel outside of the physical body into the astral world – a subtle sphere of finer than atomic forces divided into higher and lower planes of existence. The astral universe is said to be the blueprint of our material universe.

Akashic Record The history of the universe that is imprinted on the ether and which can be accessed using psychic skills.

chakras A term used in yoga for the seven centres of auric energy that run along the spine. The Indian word chakra translates as "wheel" because its energy is like a hub from which radiate rays of prana energy.

clairaudience The psychic ability to hear spirit voices.

clairsentience The psychic ability to feel spirit presence or sense psychic vibrations.

clairvoyance The psychic ability to see spirit people or see visions of the future.

cryptesthesia A dowsing term to denote the response to a "vibration" given off by water. By means of cryptesthesia knowledge of whatever object is searched for enters the dowsers subconscious mind and influences the dowsing rods by unconscious muscular reactions.

déjà vu The sense that one's witnessed some new situation or episode on a previous occasion.

Deva A Hindu word meaning "a being of light". A term adopted by the Findhorn Foundation for nature spirits that encourage the growth of plants. Each species of plant has its own Deva, i.e. Tomato Deva, Spinach Deva, etc.

dowsing Detecting water or other materials by means of divining rods or pendulum.

ESP (abbreviation for Extra Sensory Perception)
The term, coined by parapsychologist J B Rhine, refers to any mental faculty which allows a person to acquire information about the world without the use of known senses.

ether An intangible elastic substance formerly supposed to fill all space and to conduct light waves, electric waves, etc. Considered by psychics to be the medium through which telepathic thought travels.

etheric double Also known as the etheric body, duplicate body, and astral body, this is the state existing between the physical body and the aura. The etheric double is the counterpart of the human body and made of prana. It is the vehicle for astral travel.

interiorization By withdrawing the senses the awareness is focused on the inner self.

karma A Hindu term for the spiritual law of cause and effect from the Sanskrit kri, to do. Each man is considered the master of his destiny: whatever actions or thought he has set in motion return like a wheel to their starting point. The western equivalent is found in the words of Jesus: "As ye sow, so shall ye reap."

Kirlian photography A technique developed by the Russian scientist Semyon Kirlian, to photograph the aura. An object and film are placed between two metal plates charged with a powerful electrical field to obtain the picture.

mantra A holy word or phrase that is either chanted or intoned to focus concentration and raise spiritual awareness.

Nadis The yoga term for channels of the astral body through which prana energy flows. The most important run as a group of three from the base of the spine to the top of the head.

oracle A technique or person used as a means of prophecy.

overself The higher aspect of the self that exists on another plane of being. In the East it is known as Adhyatma.

prana A Hindu term for the lifeforce energy. It is the substance of the astral world and life principle of the physical world. Western spiritual healers believe it is the energy that flows through their fingers to their patient.

pranayama The conscious control of prana through breathing techniques.

precognition The psychic acquisition of information about an event before it happens.

psychokinesis The power of the mind to manipulate matter.

psychometry The psychic ability to sense the history of an object by holding it.

querant The personal consulting an oracle.

radiesthesia The use of a pendulum (or divining rod) for medical diagnosis or for finding lost objects.

remote viewing The psychic ability to witness events at a remote location without use of the known senses.

scryer The means of practising clairvoyance or divination by gazing into a crystal ball or bowl of water.

tarot A set of 78 cards used for fortune telling the origins of which are not known for certain. Some authorities believe the name originates from an anagram of the hebrew word TORA meaning natural law.

tasseography A method of fortune telling using tea leaves that probably began in ancient China.

telepathy The psychic transmission of information from one mind to another without the use of the known senses.

third-eye The psychic centre in the middle of the forehead through which clairvoyant visions are seen. Also known as the sixth chakra.

TM (abbreviation for Transcendental Meditation)
A meditation technique brought to the West by Maharishi Mahesh Yogi in 1958. This simple method employs a mantra to still the mind and trigger deep relaxation and improved alertness.

visualization A mental image used in meditation to promote inner peace or psychic powers.

watching the breath A yoga technique to still the mind by fixing the attention on the breath during meditation.

Zener cards A set of cards with simple symbols on them designed by parapsychologists J B Rhine and K Zener to statistically test ESP in the laboratory

Index